A Taste of Syria

The Hippocrene Cookbook Library

AFRICA AND OCEANIA
The Best of Regional African Cooking
Good Food from Australia
Taste of Eritrea
Traditional South African Cookery

ASIA AND MIDDLE EAST
Afghan Food and Cookery
The Art of Persian Cooking
The Art of Turkish Cooking
The Art of Uzbek Cooking
The Best of Korean Cuisine
The Best of Regional Thai Cuisine
The Best of Taiwanese Cuisine
The Cuisine of the Caucasus Mountains
Egyptian Cooking
Flavors of Burma
Healthy South Indian Cooking
Imperial Mongolian Cooking
The Indian Spice Kitchen
Japanese Home Cooking
Sephardic Israeli Cuisine
A Taste of Syria
A Taste of Turkish Cuisine

MEDITERRANEAN
The Best of Greek Cuisine, Expanded Edition
A Spanish Family Cookbook
Taste of Malta
Tastes of North Africa
Tastes of the Pyrenees, Classic and Modern

WESTERN EUROPE
The Art of Dutch Cooking, Expanded Edition
The Art of Irish Cooking
A Belgian Cookbook
Cooking in the French Fashion (bilingual)
Cuisines of Portuguese Encounters
Feasting Galore Irish-Style
The Scottish-Irish Pub and Hearth Cookbook
The Swiss Cookbook
Traditional Food from Scotland
Traditional Food from Wales
A Treasury of Italian Cuisine (bilingual)

SCANDINAVIA
The Best of Scandinavian Cooking
The Best of Finnish Cooking
The Best of Smorgasbord Cooking
Icelandic Food & Cookery
Tastes & Tales of Norway

CENTRAL EUROPE
All Along the Rhine
All Along the Danube
The Art of Hungarian Cooking
Bavarian Cooking
The Best of Austrian Cuisine
The Best of Czech Cooking
The Best of Polish Cooking
The Best of Slovak Cooking
Hungarian Cookbook
Old Warsaw Cookbook
Old Polish Traditions
Poland's Gourmet Cuisine
The Polish Country Kitchen Cookbook
Polish Heritage Cookery
Treasury of Polish Cuisine (bilingual)

EASTERN EUROPE
The Art of Lithuanian Cooking
The Best of Albanian Cooking
The Best of Croatian Cooking
The Best of Russian Cooking
The Best of Ukrainian Cuisine
Taste of Romania
Taste of Latvia
Traditional Bulgarian Cooking

AMERICAS
Argentina Cooks!
The Art of Brazilian Cookery
The Art of South American Cookery
Cooking With Cajun Women
Cooking the Caribbean Way
French Caribbean Cuisine
Mayan Cooking
Old Havana Cookbook (bilingual)
A Taste of Haiti
A Taste of Quebec

REFERENCE
International Dictionary of Gastronomy

A Taste of Syria

Virginia Jerro Gerbino
Philip M. Kayal

HIPPOCRENE BOOKS
NEW YORK

Illustrations by Anthony Gerbino
Photographs by Anthony Gerbino and Joseph Kayal

Book and jacket design by Acme Klong Design, Inc.

For more information, address:
HIPPOCRENE BOOKS, INC.
171 Madison Avenue
New York, NY 10016

ISBN 0-7818-0946-0
Cataloging-in-Publication Data available from the Library of Congress.
Printed in the United States of America.

Acknowledgments

Without relatives and friends contributing their expertise as readers and crit-cs, this book could not be completed. The same must be said of our publish-er, Hippocrene Books, and its editorial staff. A special thanks to both Carol Chitnis-Gress for accepting our book proposal and Anne McBride, our editor, or carefully nurturing this project to completion. Without her patient support and advice, we would have despaired early on.

To say that *Sitto* Helen (Virginia's mother) was taxed with questions more han anyone else is an understatement. Almost daily and sometimes three or our times a day, Virginia sought her out, if not for recipe content, then for pronunciations and spellings. As long as she did not interrupt "Jeopardy" or Wheel of Fortune" her questions were answered. *Sitto* Helen recently moved n with her other daughter Annette, who also excels in the kitchen. Not only vas she the liaison between Virginia and their mother, but a tester and proof-eader as well. Though a working grandmother herself, Annette was most upportive and patient during our endless consultations and revisions. We tip our hats to them with a special thank you.

Virginia's husband Tony endured her requests for computer assistance with utmost patience. He, and daughter Joymarie, helped out directly with the lay-out of the text and their encouragement and guidance were a source of inspi-ation. Their sons, Joseph, Anthony, and Stephen also offered encouragement, upport, and technical advice.

Of all our readers and advisors, we give special thanks to George Hayek, our butcher in Paterson, New Jersey, who we questioned for details almost as often as *Sitto* Helen. Special thanks must be given to Joe and Pat Kayal, who not only proofread but also offered countless editorial suggestions. Virginia's ousins, Marilyn Jerro Tadross and Barbara Sayour, excellent cooks themselves, offered both their recipes and expertise as did Rita and Joe Kassis who also helped in the Arabic spelling and translations. Michele Kayal Limaye, Philip's niece, often served as our tester and critic. A journalist and avid cook herself, he read and re-read parts of the book with a sharp eye and discerning palate.

Table of Contents

Introduction

Our grandparents came to America at the turn of the last century as part of the great migration from Europe and the Middle East. We wrote this book to honor them and to preserve our family cooking traditions while memories are still vivid, and our knowledgeable relatives still with us. Though we are now three generations removed from those dear pioneers, there are cherished traditions that never change, like the home cooking we grew up with.

Alice Kayal and Helen Jerro, our parents and the source of most of our recipes, are the children of George and Wadia Kassar who emigrated from Aleppo, Syria. Alice and Helen and their sister Mary excelled in the kitchen and this cookbook is written in tribute to their considerable skills. Unlike their older brothers, Nicholas, Joseph, and Camille, the girls and another brother, Bill, were born in this country. Philip's mother, Alice, married Mitchell Kayal; Helen married Richard Jerro, and Virginia, their daughter, married Anthony Gerbino. Alice and Helen, as grandmothers, were affectionately called *Sitto* in Arabic, and Mitchell and Richard, *Giddo*, for grandfather.

Over the years we spoke frequently about compiling a book of our mothers' recipes, but never sensed the urgency. Soon after Sitto Alice passed away in 1991, we felt compelled to memorialize her in some small way and pay tribute to Sitto Helen, who remains a creative cook and baker to this day. This book celebrates the gastronomic joys that were part of our childhood. Our mothers cooked from memory, but fortunately, they did write some things down. Philip found his mother's recipes, put them on a disk and mailed it to Virginia. The rest is history.

A Taste of Syria will take you across centuries and continents. By using it we hope you will better appreciate the ethnic heritage and culinary delights of all Syrian Americans. These tasty treasures are about history and culture as much as they are about good eating. Recipes help, but it took patience, reflection, observation, and hard work to acquire the skills to replicate our parents' cuisine. While we tried our best to reproduce their recipes accurately, we realize that all cooks like to improvise and add their own personal touch.

Family Traditions

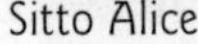

Sitto Alice

Sitto Helen

Sitto Alice was older than Sitto Helen and more traditional. But Sitto Helen would also insist on doing things her own way and there were times when neither would budge on a cooking issue. Perhaps it was age and seniority that explain their personality traits and different areas of cooking proficiency. Alice learned, from their mother, to call the chopped lamb *kabob*, while Helen preferred *kafta*, a more recent term. Sitto Helen excels at pastries. Sitto Alice made only one, *batlawa franjea*, a farina based, baked pudding. The reason for the difference in their preferences and skills will never be known. Neither ate any cheese except Syrian (*halabi*) cheese. Alice's family, the Kayals, loved stuffed meatballs (*kibbeh trabulsieh*) and ate them frequently, but Sitto Alice could never stuff them properly and relied on Sitto Helen or a neighbor for help. Once, they attempted to cook Syrian meat pies (*lahem'ajeen*) on English muffins instead of their usual homemade dough. "Over our dead bodies," we exclaimed and that was the end of it. There was a brief effort in the Syrian community in the rebellious '60s to substitute beef for lamb. Alice and Helen resisted successfully and lamb continues as the traditional meat of choice to this day.

Virginia remembers visiting her Aunt Mary as a child and watching her prepare *batlawa franjea*. Before Mary poured the pudding into the baking pan, Virginia and her cousins would beg her to leave some in the pot so they could indulge themselves unceremoniously. Licking the spoon was the best part and the uncooked pudding tasted just as good as the finished product.

In December, on the feast day of St. Barbara, our mothers would prepare *slee'ah*, a sweet dessert made with whole-wheat kernels and fresh pomegranates, which we would devour until we almost became ill. Whenever they made *cara'beech*, a delicious marshmallow covered, walnut-stuffed pastry, they would chase us to dab the topping on our foreheads or noses. Giddo Richard was notorious for this and to this day we would do the same with our own grandchildren if we could catch them.

Our families had many marvelous parties (*sah'rhas*) that seemed to go on for days. The most elaborate was the celebration of Uncle Nick's feast day. As the eldest child of the immigrant Kassars, he garnered the most respect and was considered the wisest. This was always the party of the year and his wife, our Aunt Frances (née Hakim), spent weeks preparing all our favorite foods. There would also be *fistoh* (white pistachio nuts) for us, literally by the pound. Over time, almost every recipe in this cookbook was served at these affairs. Aunt Frances was also an excellent cook and, in fact, taught our mothers how to prepare and elegantly serve many of the foods illustrated in this cookbook.

But these parties were not just about eating good food. They reflected both our culture and history. The women of the family were always willing to help. Aunts, Emily (née Attara), Angele and Jeanette (née Jerro), Mary and our mothers were always in the kitchen or serving appetizers (*mezze*) and entrées. As kids, we stood by the kitchen door waiting to grab the first taste of whatever they were bearing.

Then and now, preparing, even eating, Syrian food is a collective enterprise. It is produced in abundance and served accordingly. Almost always, all courses are served simultaneously. This allows the entire family, including mothers, to eat together—another custom that we once took for granted.

As a rule, Sittos never measure anything. They earn the privilege after years of accommodating family tastes. Rarely do they compromise or innovate. The food is always consistent. If you exclaim, as you often did, "Mom, this is delicious!" she would look surprised while affirming that she makes it "the same way every time." On a recent trip to Syria, Phil noted that the food at home had barely changed from that served in Aleppo, nearly a hundred years after the emigration.

Our fathers also cooked. Philip's dad, Giddo Mitchell, had a few specialties, namely salads, which would make your teeth ache in anticipation. His marinade for shish kabob (*mishwie*) was especially delicious. He would also place lamb bones in a large pot (*dungerrah*) covering them with any stuffed vegetable that Sitto Alice was preparing. The meat on the bones would absorb the cooking flavors and he would chew the meat right off the bone. He also thought baked rump was the best part of a chicken. What can we say?

Giddo Richard, Virginia's father, often worked in the kitchen side by side with Sitto Helen. Virginia remembers her dad preparing cured meat (*adeed*) during the winter, to the dismay of his neighbors, by hanging pieces of prime lamb or beef outdoors to dry. The result was a delicious Syrian prosciutto. Yes, we have included the recipe.

While vacationing in the Catskills during the summer months, Giddo Richard, his brother Charlie and sister Jeanette made a wonderful jelly from pink roses selected from their own gardens. The petals were cooked in a mixture of sugar, water, and lemon juice and the taste recalled the essence of perfume. It was a bit strong for some but loved by others.

Hopefully, these recipes will continue to be passed down from generation to generation for both historic and health reasons. Syrian food, quite simply, is very good for you. What could be better than fresh vegetables, olive oil, wheat, lean meat, yogurt, garlic, lemon, parsley, and unleavened bread? They are trendy now, but we used them all along.

Nothing is ever as good as mom's home cooking, but few meals can compare to those from our Sittos' Aleppian kitchens. We try to enjoy this very special cuisine every day of the year. Clearly, we love Syrian food and hope you will too.

A Brief History of Syria

The Middle East is often referred to as the "cradle of civilization." The region, with Syria at its center, connects Asia with Africa. Syria, once a province of the Roman Empire, was vulnerable to numerous invasions, but its location also made it a nexus of trade, influencing the development of western civilization and many cultures. As a crossroads, Syria exported not only food, cloth, and spices, but gave the world, especially the West, science, the alphabet, and monotheistic religion.

Syria also gave birth to agriculture and settled communities, housing Damascus and Aleppo, two of the oldest "living cities" on earth. Both were occupied long before the West was considered civilized. Cuneiform writing tablets from the Bronze Age (3000 to 2000 B.C.) have been found there. From 1600 to 539 B.C., ancient Syria was occupied primarily by Hittites, Persians, and Arameans, the source of the Aramean language, spoken by Jesus a thousand years later, and today by Maronite Catholics in both Lebanon and Syria.

The Hellenistic Empire, after Alexander the Great, dominated the Middle East from about 333 to 64 B.C., and established western rule over Syria and Palestine. The occupation combined Western and Eastern cultures but gave Syria a predominately Greek character that lasted until the Romans controlled it from 64 B.C. to nearly 400 A.D. During this period Syria quartered the earliest forms of Christianity in its deserts and mountains. Though Islam became the dominant religion after 632 A.D., Christians, as well as Jews, were well tolerated, especially under the Abbaid Dynasty (750 to 1199 A.D.). It was at this time that the Arabic language took root and became both widespread and identified with Islam. The West, believing that Islam was intolerant of Christianity, initiated the Crusades to reclaim the region for the Pope. Syria, though attacked and eventually occupied by the West, drove out the Crusaders between 1200 and 1300 A.D. It was at this time that the Krak Des Chevaliers fortress, now a tourist attraction, was built by French defenders on the road midway between Aleppo and Damascus.

The Mameluke occupation of the Fertile Crescent, as the area around Syria was known, lasted from 1250 until 1516 A.D. when the Ottoman Turks took over. Neither period was entirely positive for Syria. First, invasions from Asia distracted the Mamelukes, trade suffered, and the land lay fallow. In 1516, the Ottoman Sultan, Selim I, defeated the Mamelukes in Aleppo and proclaimed himself Caliph. Though the Ottomans encouraged road building, trade, and education and the markets or souks of Aleppo and Damascus flourished under them, much of the wealth generated by these improvements was transferred to Istanbul at Syria's expense. The Turks encouraged the building of the great mosques of Damascus and Aleppo and they still stand proudly today. Damascus flourished as the last stop on the road to Mecca for Arabs and Asians and Aleppo prospered as a trading post for Europeans into the modern period.

With the end of World War I in 1918, and the defeat of the Ottomans, Syria instituted a parliamentary government under Emir Feisal with Damascus as its capital. France and England dominated Greater Syria, giving rise to Arab nationalism—a movement by Syria and Egypt for independence from foreign control. But, under French and English mandates, the region was divided into current-day Syria and Lebanon (French), while Palestine and Jordan went to the British. King Feisal was made king of Iraq.

Syria was further divided by the French into the provinces of Aleppo, Damascus, Latakia, and Hauran. As semi-independent city-states, however, they again became part of Syria by 1942. In 1946 Lebanon, a semi-autonomous district under the Maronite Catholics, moved for independence from both the West and Syria. As a result of the French occupation, many Syrians also speak French. Arabic, nonetheless, remains the dominant language, outnumbering resident speakers of Aramaic and Syriac, two other ancient languages of the region.

Modern Syria is thus a product of both Western and Eastern civilizations. It is at the intersection of the world of commerce and religion, drawing from and adding to the great traditions of Asia, Africa and Europe. Though it is a mixture of races and nationalities that have blended into one people and one nation, its predominant culture and language is Arabic. Syria today is home to many displaced Turks, Kurds, Palestinians, and Lebanese. It has long had prosperous and resident Jewish and Armenian communities that remain supported and protected by state law.

As visitors to Syria often note, it is impossible to get from one place to the next without stumbling over a Roman ruin. Yet, as an American tourist destination, Syria is a best-kept secret. While the country is safe, inexpensive, and beautiful, and the ruins of Palmyra are as fascinating as the souks of Aleppo and the mosques of Damascus, for us, its highly acclaimed cuisine and its friendly population are its major attraction.

Syrians in America

At the beginning of the twentieth century, most of the "Arabs" arriving in America were Christians from the region of Mount Lebanon and the cities of Syria. With them came Jews from Aleppo who settled mainly in Brooklyn, New York. Like many immigrants, they identified themselves by their towns rather than their country of origin. Our grandparents, for example, called themselves "Aleppians." In time, they became Syrians, although assimilated European Americans often held this identity against them because Syrians were thought to be non-white Asians or Muslims. Proud of our lineage, identity, and accomplishments, we identify ourselves today as both Syrian and Arab. Our immediate ancestors, however, were most comfortable using religious identities like Melkite and Maronite (Eastern-rite Catholics) or as Eastern Orthodox Christians should they be of that faith. Even though our parents and grandparents rarely identified themselves publicly as Arabs, they would always inquire in Arabic whether someone to whom they were introduced was "ibn Arab" or "bint Arab?"—son or daughter of an Arab.

To complicate the question of identity, Syria, and then Lebanon, became separate nations after our grandparents arrived in America and, in time, the Syrian-American community split in two. Many American Syrians became Lebanese and the community here became known as "Syrian-Lebanese." But, food, bread, music, and, language (though erroneous) continued to be referred to as Syrian. Eventually, however, our beloved Syrian bread evolved into "*pita*" and our food is now often referred to as "Middle Eastern" or "Mediterranean" by trendy restaurateurs. Perhaps, this is how it should be since, over time, many ethnic groups have adopted elements of this cuisine. Also, emigrants are still arriving here from Lebanon, Palestine, Jordan, and Egypt, so continuing to apply Syrian as the primary identifier for bread, food, and music, would be inappropriate.

If Syrian Christians were the first "Arabs" to come to America, this is no longer the case. Since 1965, thousands of other Arabic speakers have come to these shores in search of a better life. Unlike the earlier immigrants, these later arrivals are more likely to be Muslim and better educated. They are also less likely to be entrepreneurial. The Syrians in America were famed as peddlers, bringing hard gotten goods to isolated American communities. Once they settled down, they became dry good store owners, merchants, and manufacturers, concentrating their energies in the garment and shoe industries.

The Syrians were very successful in business, producing in 1910 a Syrian Business Directory that listed all Syrian businesses in this country. They, thus, helped one another succeed. Historians often note that "they arrived in the middle class." Their hard earned wealth and affluence guaranteed their total and rapid assimilation into the American mainstream. Today, they are educators, doctors, lawyers, and successful participants in all American institutions and industries, from government and the military to Wall Street.

While many of these newer Middle Eastern groups are widely dispersed throughout the United States (like the Syrians are now), many prefer the security and comfort of living among similar others. They bring with them rich and diversified traditions that enhance our nation's multi-cultural heritage. The old Syrian enclave of Paterson, New Jersey, for example, almost entirely from Aleppo, Syria, is now populated by Palestinians and Jordanians. They have enlivened the downtown business district and have added a touch of the "old country," reviving memories for the assimilated Syrians who used to live there in "little Syria" around Main Street. What keeps the suburban Syrian ethnically conscious is their religious traditions and the occasional visit "downtown" to see where *giddo* and *sitto* originally lived. The same is true in Brooklyn, New York and in Boston, Massachusetts where colorful cafes, Arab shops, dry good stores, and restaurants now abound.

Sharing a language, all these populations are bound together by a common culture, including music, dance and food. Arabic-speaking people are known for their hospitality, love of family, and respect for education. Yet, each national groups has its unique traditions and culinary specialties. Even the same meal in any two countries may be titled (if not pronounced) differently. Syrians, for example, call grape leaves *yebrat*, while the Lebanese call the same meal, *warak in'ib*.

Given this ethnic diversity from the same region, it is no surprise that within our own ethnic group, each province, city, town, and family would also have their own variations of the recipes in this book. So try everything, improvise and make modifications that suit your own taste.

We tried our best, with some difficulty, to emulate Sitto Helen's pronunciation of the Arabic words in each recipe. We recognize, of course, that her pronunciation is idiomatic and may not be universally recognized as correct. The spellings are our phonetic translations. Ease of reading and understanding directions were our main concern. We hope we have succeeded.

The Cuisine of Aleppo

To understand Syrian cuisine as it developed in Aleppo, our family's hometown, a little history is necessary. Aleppo is ancient, but its roots are buried beneath a very modern city. Legend has it that the prophet Abraham paused in Aleppo to milk his cows on Citadel Hill, thus spawning its Arabic name *Halab*, which means "milk." It is one of Syria's principle cities and the second largest after Damascus. Located in northwest Syria, it borders on Turkey and is at the crossroads of great and historic commercial routes, only sixty miles from the Mediterranean Sea and the Euphrates River. Aleppo lies along the Baghdad-Istanbul railway and is linked by rail with Damascus and Beirut, Lebanon. With road connections to Damascus, Latakia, and Antioch, Turkey, it is a natural gateway to Asia.

The old city of Aleppo is centered around and dominated by a twelfth-century citadel where the ancient souks, or bazaars, are found. They run along narrow and winding streets and virtually everything from spices and silks to brass are sold in these precursors to modern shopping malls.

Mezze

The city was originally laid out in walled districts entered via *babs* or doors. Different groups, such as Jews and Armenians, lived in these distinct quarters. Though no longer segregated residential entities, these areas are still known by their ethnic names. The overwhelming majority of Aleppians are Muslim, but Christians, Jews, Turks and Armenians have had a say in the life of the city for centuries. While some group rivalries exist, it is not unusual to find churches and mosques abutting one another in Syria's major cities.

Travelers in Syria quickly realize that the people are multilingual, diverse and very much aware of the diversity around them. In the crossroads that is Aleppo, this is particularly true. Like Damascus, it is filled with many foreigners, tourists, and refugees. The Ottoman occupation of Syria, Lebanon, Greece, and Armenia supplied a context for tolerance and sharing, giving Aleppians a commonality of food, albeit in slightly different forms and presentations. When we hear baklava, for example, we think of Greece, but it is also a Syrian pastry called *batlawa*. Over time, the string cheese brought to Syria by the Armenians became known as *Halabi* cheese or the cheese of Aleppo because that is where so many of these refugees settled.

For these reasons, the cuisine of Aleppo is considered by many to be not only unique, but the best of the Arab world (see "Aleppo's Allure," *The New York Times Magazine*, July 15, 1990). A mixture of Turkish, Greek, Armenian, and Arab influences, its variety and seasonings distinguish Aleppian food from all others. Aleppians serve particularly tasty versions of *kabob*, *kibbeh*, *mezze*, and stuffed vegetables. The city is famous for its hot peppers, pomegranates, and pistachio nuts. Aleppo is surrounded by flocks of fat-tailed Awassi sheep, olives and fruit orchards and its traditional dishes draw their character from its countryside. Its famous pistachios are used in many pastries, smothered in sugar syrup.

It is not only the rich assortment of appetizers, main courses and desserts that set Aleppo's cuisine apart from the rest of Syria, but attention to detail, subtlety of flavor, and elegance of presentation. Aleppo has a French ambience, while Damascus is more British. In addition, each city has its own specialties. *Mamuneh'ya*, a sweet breakfast delight, is served only in Aleppo, while a range of unique chickpea salads are commonplace in Damascus.

For appetizers, side dishes, or even a snack or luncheon meal, nothing surpasses *hummus* (puréed chickpeas) or *baba ghanouj* (puréed eggplant) with parsley or cumin as a garnish. *M'hammara*, a mix of red peppers, walnuts and pomegranate syrup, tastes great on pita. Like *lebaneh*, a yogurt spread drizzled with olive oil and dried mint, it is an appealing party dip. All these are common throughout the Middle East and vary in taste and texture from city to city and family to family.

Kibbeh trabulsieh, a popular entrée, named after the city of Tripoli, is an egg-shaped lamb and wheat meatball, stuffed with sautéed ground lamb, spices, and pine nuts. Cooked in rendered butter, it is loved by all. Likewise, *shish kabob* or *mishwie*, as we call it, is all the rage. Though our parents would eat it only with grilled onions, we now add a variety of vegetables to the skewer. The present fashion is to serve it over rice. *Mishwie* can be found on grills throughout Syria, day and night. The aroma of lamb and the scent of the ubiquitous jasmine fill the night air, especially in Damascus and Aleppo where no one dines before 10:00 p.m.

Syrians often make rice with vermicelli, sautéed in butter and cooked with chicken broth. Many serve it with lightly browned pine nuts as a garnish but it can also be made with saffron, which colors it an appealing yellow and provides a characteristic taste. Sitto Alice added only saffron to her rice; Sitto Helen only vermicelli. Both variations are very Syrian.

All Syrian food should be eaten with Syrian bread (*pita*). Finding a good bakery is important. Most large cities with Arab communities have them and we strongly recommend freshly baked Syrian bread over that sold in supermarkets. Use the bread to wipe your dish clean. Or open it and scoop up *leban, hummus, baba ghanouj* or *m'hammara*. Use it for sandwiches. Toast it for use in salads or stuff it with Syrian cheese, toasting it until the cheese melts. Delicious!

Halaweh or *halvah*, as it is called in the United States is a well-known Middle Eastern delicacy sold in many supermarkets. A combination of sesame paste, sugar, and oil it is marketed as a candy—plain, with chocolate, or with pistachios. Virginia and her children like it in pita.

A typical Syrian breakfast consists of some combination of sliced cucumber, *lebaneh* dip, Syrian cheese, olives, pita, perhaps toasted, or some *mamuneh'ya* served with cheese and pita. *Ca'ak*, a cookie and/or *arras*, a bread, with apricot jelly, Syrian cheese, and melon is also served. Aromatically flavored *za'atar* bread can also be accompanied by olives and string cheese. The beverage of choice in the morning and throughout the day would be *ah'weh turkieh*, a thick espresso heavily flavored with sugar.

In the summer, yogurt mixed with garlic slivers, mint, cucumber, and chopped lettuce makes a tantalizing lunch. Fried eggplant and/or fried squash in pita is also a summer specialty as is *ta'bouleh*, a salad consisting of parsley, scallions, wheat, dried mint, tomatoes, lemon juice, and spices. For the winter, *makhlootha* and *rhisthaya* are appealingly hearty soups as is *kibbeh lebanneya* (*kibbeh* balls in warm yogurt with rice). A full dinner menu might consist of *yebrat* (meat-stuffed grape leaves), *kibbeh trabulsieh*, or *jaj zatoon ou riz* (chicken and olives with rice) served with *ta'bouleh*. Feasts fit for a king! There are also superb meatless meals (*syamee*) for the health conscious.

It is the pastries of Aleppo that distinguish it as a world-class culinary center, especially its *gh'raybeh*, *batlawa*, and *ca'ak bil adgweh*. When made correctly, *gh'raybeh* is light and buttery, delicate to the touch and palate, beautifully pear-shaped and garnished with a sliver of pistachio or almond. Unlike the Greek version that uses honey, Syrian *batlawa* is made with sugar syrup, perhaps laced with rose water or orange blossom. *Batlawa franjea*, derived from the French occupation, is a delicious farina custard rich in butter and sprinkled with cinnamon. Desserts are served with Turkish coffee followed by *arat*, a strong Anisette liqueur. Almost all Syrian pastries can be eaten by hand. Sitto Helen is legendary for her desserts especially *gh'raybeh* and *cara-beech*.

In the middle of Aleppo, *babs* lead to the old Armenian or Christian quarter where the best pastries are found. Turks, Syrians, Greeks, and Armenians share a similar cuisine, but the Armenian influence on Aleppo's pastries is especially strong. Oddly, it is very difficult to find coffee and pastries served by the same vendors. Pastry and coffee shops usually stand side by side to serve the many Syrian families strolling for dessert each evening.

As mentioned, Syrian food in America is often referred to as Mediterranean. Many restaurants serve variations of all the appetizers we list. Everyone doctors these recipes to fit their own tastes. Unfortunately, many lose their originality and authenticity in the process—an inevitable outcome in the melting pot of America.

Many Syrian entrées have now become *mezze* (appetizers). With hosts and guests wishing to try everything, many main courses are now served as cocktail party finger foods. *Kibbeh nayeh* (lamb tartare) and *yebrat* are good examples. *Sau'seejaw* (sausage) served in lemon juice from a chafing dish with pita becomes a Syrian "pig in a blanket." There is also Giddo Richard's wonderfully cured *adeed* that can be rolled with olives and secured with a toothpick.

Zwaz (fried lamb brain) is a delicacy we loved as youngsters. Now hard to find, the lamb brains were mixed with olive oil, lemon juice, parsley and spices and served as a salad with pita on the side. It was also served in pita with lettuce as a topping. One can also add eggs and spices to the lamb brains and fry them as individual omelets, similar to *ir'jeh*. Lamb tongue, liver, and kidneys were also delicacies prepared by our parents. Though we enjoyed them, these organ foods are no longer popular because of their fat content.

Locating Foodstuffs

Any large American city has Arab, Armenian, Turkish or Greek communities that carry Middle Eastern foodstuffs. In addition to Detroit, Brooklyn, Miami, Los Angeles and Boston, cities such as Paterson, Jersey City, Cleveland, Manchester, Pawtucket, and Worcester, to name a few, have thriving Arab business districts that feature specialty stores. Fortunately, American supermarkets, especially those identified as international or gourmet, carry some basics, as do many health food stores. Pistachios, pita, *b'har* (allspice) chickpeas, fava beans, and *tahini* are commonly available items. Some of the spices can be mixed at home and many items can be purchased through mail order.

For New Yorkers, the Mid-East Grocery at 7923 Third Avenue in Brooklyn specializes in Syrian cuts of lamb. Nearby is the Mid-East Bakery at 7808 Third Avenue, an excellent source for Syrian (pita) bread, as is the Damascus Bakery on Atlantic Avenue in downtown Brooklyn. Sahadi Brothers also on Atlantic Avenue is nationally known and carries virtually everything needed to prepare a Middle Eastern meal, as do Fattal's and Nouri's bakeries in Paterson, New Jersey. George's Market on Getty Avenue in Paterson is our top choice for quality lamb. Many other Middle Eastern products are also sold there.

Middle Eastern stores can also be found on Mt. Auburn Street in Watertown, Massachusetts and the Squirrel Hill and Strip districts of Pittsburgh, Pennsylvania. In Phoenix, Arizona, you can try the Spice Bazaar and in New Orleans, the Jerusalem Restaurant and Delicatessen. Atlanta, Georgia is home to the well-known Salam's Food and Deli. The Daily Bread Marketplace in Miami, Florida carries a full line of Middle Eastern and Greek foods. Queens, New York is now home to numerous Middle Eastern groups who have established their own markets on Steinway Street in Astoria. The same has happened in Fairview, New Jersey on Anderson Avenue.

Both Detroit and Dearborn, Michigan, are home to extremely large, though not necessarily Syrian, Arab communities. In Detroit, a good place to start is the Amana Market on Fullerton. Popular stores in Dearborn are Saad Brothers' Supermarket and Harb's Imports. Both are located on West Warren Street.

Massachusetts is dotted with Syrian Lebanese communities, especially the city of Boston and its suburbs. We recommend the Cedar's Market, Byblos Restaurant, and Homsy's Café and Fresh Food Emporium in Norwood for groceries, and meats. In West Roxbury, there is Jay's Meat Market, the Nea East Bakery, Bayeh Market, and Samia Bakery, the latter known for its spinach and meat pies. For a good selection of groceries, there is Droubi Bakery in Roslindale.

Syrian cheese (block form) was made at home from rennet tablets that were commonly sold in drug or health food stores. For unknown reasons they have disappeared from the market. However, the cheese can be bought ready-made in Middle Eastern grocery stores. If you prefer homemade cheese, we have been advised that tablets can be purchased directly from the New England Cheesemaking Supply Co., 292 Main Street, Ashfield, MA 01330, or cal (413) 628-3808.

The above-mentioned items and much more can also be purchased on line An Internet search of Middle Eastern groceries offers many references to mar kets throughout the United States. Often this search will lead to Halal mar kets as well. The web site and mailing addresses for two New York supplier are: www.sultansdelight.com, Sultan's Delight, P.O. Box 090302, Brooklyn New York 11209, or call (800) 852-5046 or fax to (718) 745-2563 www.sahadi.com, Sahadi Brothers, 187 Atlantic Avenue, Brooklyn, New York or call (718) 624-4550. Fattal's at 977 Main Street in Paterson, New Jerse 07503 has recently gone online as well. Check www.fattals.com or call (973 742-7125.

Other on-line sites that offer Middle Eastern food products are www.aviso.net, www.mtofolive.com, www.salimsfood.com/grocery.htm www.elfanar.com, and www.waitrose.com. One site, www.awo.net/commerce/industry/mefoodus.asp, locates groceries by state and references smaller towns and cities.

Lamb Preparation

American butchers generally do not know how to cut or prepare lamb for Syrian or Middle Eastern cooking, so you will need a Middle Eastern butcher for this. However, you may occasionally find a neighborhood butcher who would be willing to learn.

There are three basic cuts of Syrian meat: *hubra*, *mafroomah*, and *kafta*. All Syrian cuts of meat come from the leg. *Hubra* (for *kibbeh*) should be taken from the leanest part of the leg and ground extremely fine. This is done by putting the meat through a very fine "grinder plate" twice. It should appear both smooth and red. *Mafroomah* is fattier, more coarse, and lumpy while *kafta* is in between. *Mafroomah* is made by putting the meat through a plate with large openings, and *kafta* through a plate with medium openings. When asking for *mafroomah*, or *kafta*, feel free to ask for leaner cuts.

Supermarket butchers often are willing to grind up a leg of lamb, but they will not distinguish between *mafroomah* and *kafta*. This need not be a problem, just ask for ground lamb. The *hubra* for *kibbeh* can be made from lean *shish kabob* cubes that an American market may have available.

Many American cities now have Halal markets. These are Islamic markets serving new and growing Muslim communities. Those from Arab countries will be able to prepare some of the meat discussed above, but not the *hubra* for *kibbeh* unless the butcher is from Syria or Lebanon or you explain how to do it.

Fud'dalu!
(Eat well, and enjoy!)

Glossary:

Addis	dry lentils
Adg'weh	dates
Ah'weh	coffee
A'jeen	bread dough
Asfoor	saffron (used to color and flavor food); since saffron is very expensive turmeric may be substituted.
Bana'doora	tomato
B'har	allspice (pimento tree berry)
Burghol	bulgur wheat; #1 small; #4 large
Chemen	fenugreek
Da'ah	combination of cardamom, cloves, nutmeg, allspice, black pepper, and cinnamon
Dibs Rim'an	pure pomegranate molasses
Fillo dough	fine pastry sheets
Fistoh	pistachio nuts
Halaweh/Halvah	sesame treat/candy
Hash'weh	basic meat and rice stuffing
Hebit il Baraky	black caraway seeds
Hubra	plain, leanest cut of ground lamb for all kinds of *kibbeh* meals
Humta	large whole wheat kernels used exclusively in *slee'ah*
Irfeh	cinnamon
Jib'neh	cheese
Kabob	term used for "skewed" foods; Syrian lamb burgers
Kafta	ground lamb for stuffing, etc.
Kamoon	ground cumin
Kataifi	shredded fillo dough
Khob'iz	Syrian bread/pita

Kusbara	ground coriander
Lahmeh	meat (lamb)
Leban	yogurt
Maelzahar	orange blossom water
Mafroomah	coarse chopped lamb mainly used for stuffing vegetables
Mahlab	crushed black cherry pits
Maward	distilled rose water
Mezze	appetizers; equivalent of smorgasbord
Mishwie	*shish kabob*
Nah'nah	fresh or dried mint
Pita	Syrian bread
Roh'beir	"starter" yogurt
Sa'nobar	pine or pignolia nuts
Shumrah	fennel seed
Simsum	sesame seed or sesame pita
Smeed	semolina, light yellow in color
Tahini	ground hulled sesame seeds
Tha'ah	sausage casing
Toom	garlic
Za'atar	mixture of wild oregano, thyme, sesame seeds, and sumac
Zatoon	olives
Zibdeh Migleha	rendered butter

Basic Guidelines

Read each recipe thoroughly before proceeding.

Meat

- All our entrées and appetizers are made with lamb. Some relatives toy with the occasional use of beef but we feel the meals are much tastier (and more authentic) with lamb. Beef, garlic and lemon, for some reason, do not seem to compliment each other.

  Several cuts of lamb are indicated in our recipes. *Hubra*, the leanest cut, is for *martadala* (a lamb roll) and *kibbeh* (lamb and wheat) recipes exclusively. *Kafta* is somewhat coarse and used in Syrian *kabobs* and stuffings. *Mafroomah* is a very coarse cut used in stuffing grape leaves (*yebrat*), and other vegetables. When *mafroomah* is indicated, discard any hard pieces of fat before using.

- When preparing *kibbeh nayeh* (lamb tartare) salt lightly and mix to keep blood/juices inside. Wet your hands lightly with cold water a few times while mixing. We specify ¾ cup of wheat to 1 pound *hubra* when preparing *kibbeh nayeh*. If you prefer a "grainy" texture, use more wheat. All *kibbeh* recipes start out in the form of *kibbeh nayeh*.

  For baked, stuffed *kibbeh* (flat or round) pour a small amount of butter over the *kibbeh* before freezing.

- Most everything Syrian remains flavorful the next day because the highly-seasoned sauces are absorbed by the foods. The same is true of pastries and their butter content.

- There are two types of Syrian sausage. One is *sau'seejaw*, made with pine nuts and spices and the other *simaneth*, made with chickpeas, rice and spices. We recommend sheep casings for the thinner sausage and hog casings for the wider. These casings, or *tha'ah* as we call them, can be purchased at most Middle Eastern markets or other ethnic markets where sausage is sold. They are purchased in bulk and must be separated individually before placing in a jar filled with kosher salt. After separating, wrap each skin around your finger. Remove, then wrap the end around the skin so that it does not open. The tools to stuff the skins vary in size. For the *sau'seejaw*, use a narrow opening and for the *simaneth* a wider one. KitchenAid has stuffing attachments available for its heavy-duty mixer. We are not sure of the full range, but it is worth looking into.

- When cooking stuffed vegetables, such as grape leaves, cabbage, eggplant, and squash, we recommend using a wide, deep pot. We do not recommend stuffing vegetables the day before cooking because they tend to get soggy. When scooping out eggplant and squash for stuffing, do not discard the innards. They can be cooked in the pot with the vegetables or prepared as a side dish to a meat or fish entrée. Just cook in tomato sauce until tender or in water with butter, salt, and pepper.

  Lamb bones can be cooked in the same pot with stuffed vegetables. We suggest using bones from the shoulder because they are meatier than the ones from the leg. Rinse and remove visible fat before placing into the pot. The bones absorb the juices and are delicious prepared this way. If lamb bones are not used, we recommend using a vegetable steamer basket under the stuffed vegetables to protect the bottom layer from overcooking.

  Also, after the vegetables are cooked, close the heat, tilt the cover, and pour the juices into a bowl. Use the juices to reheat leftovers. If freezing, pour some of the juices over the vegetables. Stuffed zucchini, peppers, potatoes, and tomatoes can be cooked together in the same pot. If you choose to do this, place the tomatoes and peppers on top of the other vegetables, since they tend to cook faster.

  If you prefer vegetarian cuisine, any combination of fresh, chopped vegetables with rice can be substituted for meat when stuffing vegetables, including grape leaves.

- When a recipe specifies "soak wheat," simply place the wheat into a bowl or large measuring cup, cover with cold water, stir, and immediately drain and refrigerate. For *kibbeh nayeh* we recommend refrigerating the wheat for 30 minutes before using. If you soak wheat longer, it expands and will not be appropriate for this use.

Pastries

- Rendered butter is preferred over sweet, unsalted butter for use in pastries and some entrées. We recommend using salted sweet cream butter for rendering because of its unique flavor. If time is limited, unsalted butter may be substituted, but do not tell Sitto Helen! She will not approve. Unused rendered butter can be refrigerated for months. If a recipe does not specify rendered butter, use salted, sweet cream butter.

- You can blend meat mixtures or dough for pastries in a heavy-duty mixer. When mixing meat do so until just blended. Dough will have to be mixed longer on low speed.

- When "preheated oven" is specified, do so for approximately 15 minutes at 350 degrees, unless otherwise indicated.

- Place pastries or cookies on ungreased baking pans/cookie sheets and rotate the pans occasionally for even browning.

- To maintain freshness, fillo dough must be refrigerated. Remove from the refrigerator at least ½ hour before using. Carefully pick up the sheets with two hands since they tend to rip easily. The dough can be purchased in Middle Eastern stores or at local supermarkets. While we recommend fresh, frozen is also available; just thaw in the refrigerator overnight. Since the dough dries out quickly, we suggest covering with plastic wrap while using. The objective is to prevent air from contacting the dough. A lightly damp towel can also be used but plastic wrap is a bit more effective.

- If a recipe indicates nuts as an ingredient, we suggest buying them shelled. We also recommend that you double-check for shell fragments before using. If using pistachios and/or almonds, the skins should be removed, unless otherwise indicated. To do this, blanche the nuts by bringing cold water in a saucepan to a boil. Add the nuts; lower the heat and simmer for 2 minutes. Drain the water and remove the skins immediately. Nuts contain their own oils so when browning, it is not necessary to add butter or oil to the pan.

- Use granulated sugar in dessert recipes unless otherwise specified. If a recipe indicates sugar syrup as an ingredient, use at room temperature.

- Use all natural vanilla extract in dessert recipes.

- Use **pressed** dates when dates are specified in a recipe. American supermarkets do not usually sell dates packaged this way, but they can be purchased in most Middle Eastern stores. Though a package may state pitted, for some reason pits are always found, so it is important to check before using. Virginia advises using disposable gloves when doing this, otherwise dates stick to your hands and it can be quite messy. Rub some melted butter on the gloves so that the dates do not stick to them.

- While rapid-rise yeast may work, we only use active dry yeast for dough recipes.

- When preparing dough for pastries add extra flour if the dough feels too soft and does not hold together when rolling. To prevent the dough from drying out when preparing meat or spinach pies, cover the pieces with a light-colored cloth or towel.

- Sitto Helen prefers Heckers flour for baking. Use unbleached, all-purpose flour throughout.

Miscellaneous/Advice

- When soaking wheat for *ta'bouleh* or any salad, do not drain the water; leave the wheat soaking for approximately one hour. Squeeze tightly before using to remove excess water. It is not necessary to refrigerate the wheat used for these salads. Be aware, *burghol* (wheat) comes in sizes 1 through 4; 1 being the smallest and 4 the largest.

- Virtually all entrées, appetizers, soups, cheeses, and desserts can be frozen. However, we do not recommend freezing *shibiat* (fillo pastry with ricotta filling) or *batlawa franjea* (baked farina pudding). After thawing and reheating, the texture is not the same as freshly baked. Also, be sure foods/desserts are properly wrapped before freezing.

- A variety of meals and desserts can be partially prepared the day before, such as boiling chickens or cabbage; scooping out vegetables before stuffing; rinsing, drying and chopping parsley, lettuce, onions, garlic and other vegetables, or shelling and chopping nuts for pastries. Use your own judgment.

Commonly known as pita, Syrian bread has become very popular. Our experience, however, is that many people do not know how to use it correctly. They fail to open it and instead use it closed. Essentially, it is a pocket bread that can be halved or quartered, then opened and used accordingly.

When serving with Syrian food, such as *kibbeh nayeh* (lamb tartare), *hummus* (puréed chickpeas), *sau'seejaw* (lamb sausage), cut the loaves into quarters before placing into a breadbasket, then protect from the air to keep fresh. You can use the bread opened to scoop appetizers; wipe the juices off your plate, especially after eating *coussa mahshee* (lamb stuffed squash) or *yebrat* or, just eat it plain. If you wish a crispier bread for scooping up appetizers, *m'hammara* (red pepper dip) in particular, pita chips work just fine. Almost all entrées, breakfast dishes, appetizers, soups, and/or salads are served with Syrian bread.

Today's popular round loaves are much smaller than years ago. When a loaf was passed around the table, you would pull off a piece for yourself. Today, each diner gets his/her own personal loaf. Americans, of course, prefer utensils so it is acceptable to open the bread and put the *kibbeh*, *hummus*, *baba ghanouj* (puréed eggplant), *sau'seejaw*, etc. into it with a spoon or fork. The old-timers simply pick up these items with one scoop. For sandwiches, just partially open a loaf along the edge or cut one in half and stuff with whatever you wish.

Simsum bread is another type of pita that is thicker than regular pita and covered with sesame seeds. It is delicious plain or with cold cuts, but is not available in American markets. Ideally, the best pita is bought from Middle Eastern bakeries. The supermarket variety tends to be drier, harder and often has a chemical taste. Syrian bread should be pliable and smell freshly baked.

Pita freezes quite well. Just double-bag it. If you are in a rush, you can remove one pita at a time, place in a low-temperature oven for a minute or so and it will be ready to use. You can also place a sheet of paper towel around the bread and thaw in a microwave oven for approximately 10 seconds. Pita can also thaw naturally in a plastic bag in 10 to 15 minutes. To prevent it from drying (and it does so quickly if exposed to air) leave the bread in a closed plastic bag until ready to eat. Do not put warm pita in a plastic bag, it will get soggy.

- Kosher salt is used in all recipes. It has a coarse texture and is a bit more potent than regular salt.

- When using tahini (sesame paste) to make hummus or baba ghanouj, etc., stir well. For ease of stirring, turn the tahini jar upside down for an hour or two before mixing.

- All special utensils/tools needed to stuff sausages, prepare *ir'jeh* (parsley and egg omelets) decorate pastries, etc., can be purchased in Middle Eastern markets. Coring devices are needed to remove the innards of squash, eggplant, and other vegetables. After the stem ends are removed, an open cylinder similar to that used in the preparation of cannoli is inserted in the vegetable, turned, and retracted. The tube should have the innards in it. Use a dowel to clean out the cylinder.

  Originally, a cylinder was rolled into shape from flattened aluminum with one seam placed over the other to form a sharp edge. When inserted and turned, it would cut the innards off the sides of the vegetables. We doubt if these tubes can still be bought in this country, but a cannoli tube works fairly well. Sophisticated stores selling kitchenwares have elongated scrapers, used to scrape the sides clean, as will any Middle Eastern or East Indian markets.

- Canola oil and all-vegetable shortening are recommended for frying. Olive oil is recommended for meat/vegetable mixtures, salads, etc. A range of olive oils is now available in markets. We recommend using a full-bodied olive oil on *kibbeh nayeh* and in *hummus* and *baba ghanouj*. The type of oil to use for frying, salads, etc. is, of course, a personal choice.

- Realemon bottled lemon juice is recommended for cooking stuffed grape leaves and a variety of other stuffed vegetables. Use 1-cup lemon juice for each pound of meat, and add water so the mixture covers at least ½ of the vegetables.

- Do not rinse rice before cooking; the nutritional value diminishes. Also when preparing, use a heavy, wide, deep pot for best results. Our Sittos prefer Carolina long-grain rice. The only time Sitto Helen uses Uncle Ben's rice is when she prepares turkey stuffing. No explanation! If we specify serve with Syrian rice either rice with vermicelli or rice with saffron or turmeric may be used. It is your choice.

- Use curly American parsley only when decorating a platter. Flat Italian parsley is used primarily as an ingredient in recipes. When using fresh parsley, remove stems, rinse and dry well on paper towels before chopping. We recommend fresh parsley exclusively.

  Syrians use large quantities of chopped parsley in sauces and meals such as *ir'jeh* or *ta'bouleh*. Use the following measurements as a guide: 1 small bunch equals ½ cup, 1 medium bunch, 1 cup, and 1 large bunch, 1½ cups.

  When preparing *fatayer sabinech* (spinach pies/triangles) or *sambousak* (lamb turnovers), we recommend spreading the dough with a rolling pin.

  We recommend removing the seeds from fresh tomatoes before dicing. When using canned, peeled, whole tomatoes, or stewed tomatoes, crush by hand (we feel the taste and consistency of canned crushed tomatoes are not as good). Other than in recipes requiring a tomato sauce and lemon mixture (mainly for cooking stuffed vegetables), it is fine to substitute freshly diced tomatoes or stewed tomatoes.

  When dry lentils are specified in a recipe check for small stones before using.

- Pomegranate or "Chinese apple" is a fruit with a tough reddish rind and many seeds enclosed in a juicy red pulp. The fruit is available in late summer through the early part of winter. We use the seeds as a garnish for appetizers and in *slee'ah* (whole-wheat dessert). To remove them, cut the fruit in quarters; break apart the pieces and hand pick the seeds. This can be quite messy (wear an apron) because the seeds "squirt," so we suggest placing the pieces in a deep bowl set in the sink before proceeding.

- Syrians use quite a bit of *nah'nah* (dried mint) in their cooking. Mint goes well with lamb and is a central ingredient in many meals. It is best home grown or can be purchased from a Middle Eastern market. The dried mint sold in American grocery stores is acceptable but the quantity sold in a single container is not enough to enhance the taste of a meal of stuffed vegetables. It is also less expensive to buy in bulk.

  When home grown mint has matured, snip the vines near the base. When cut, mint grows back almost immediately and spreads abundantly. Wash thoroughly until all the dirt is removed. Drain in a colander. To remove the leaves, slide your fingers down the stem to the bottom. Also, clip off the leaves at the very top and use.

To dry, place the leaves on paper towels or newspapers and turn them over occasionally. The drying process should take a few days. Once they are completely dry, grab a handful, and rub them back and forth through a fine strainer or through the holes in a colander. A flaky, near powdery consistency results. Discard stem pieces and place into a tight container or plastic bag.

- Use proper measuring utensils, not the spoons and cups you eat with.
- When a large amount of crushed garlic is specified for stuffed vegetables, we recommend using a mortar and pestle or a garlic press. If using a mortar and pestle, add some kosher salt and mint to the garlic and then mash. Partially cover the mortar with your free hand to prevent the mixture from splashing.
- We have provided recipes for vegetarian meals that can be served at different times of the day and in different venues. Also, certain appetizers, luncheon meals, salads, and soups can be served as entrées or side dishes. Recommended side dishes are, of course, optional.
- Syrians, especially those from Aleppo, often use a thick pomegranate molasses to flavor some meat mixtures. It can be bought prepared in any Middle Eastern store and in some gourmet markets. We have included an Americanized version (page 185) that is easy to prepare at home. Once made, it can be refrigerated for months on end.
- In a few of our recipes, we specify "cover with a heavy cloth or towel." This is to keep the item at room temperature and prevent hardening.
- Please note that yield approximations vary according to size or portion.
- Fresh grape leaves are preferred over store bought and small to medium-size leaves are best for stuffing. Middle Eastern and Greek markets sell bottled grape leaves and/or fresh leaves from barrels but we feel the leaves freshly picked from the vine, offer the best texture and taste. Planted near a trestle or fence, grapevines flourish well with minimal effort. If you wish to plant one, check with your local nursery.

To prepare the leaves for cooking, gently remove the stems and stack the leaves seam side up. If you have a kitchen scale, weigh them and separate into ½-pound packages. Rinse the leaves under cold water and shake excess water off. Tie loosely with thread or string, crisscross fashion. Place in a pot of boiling water for a few minutes or until the leaves turn a brownish/green color. It may be necessary to hold the leaves down with a large spoon to keep them immersed. Remove carefully with a large slotted spoon and place in a colander to drain and cool. Squeeze gently (do not twist); open and lay flat. The leaves may be used immediately or frozen for later use.

If using bottled grape leaves, rinse well under cold water; squeeze gently and remove the stems.

Sukh'tane!
(Glad you enjoyed your meal!)

Breakfast
(Ef'tour)

APRICOT JELLY

Mishmoosh *Yield: Approximately eight 8-ounce canning jars*

Apricots, like pistachios, are native to the Middle East. American supermarkets sell two varieties. One is light orange in color and soft. We recommend the other, slightly darker and firm, and packaged by Sun Maid as California apricots. They can also be purchased in large quantities, at a more reasonable price, at Sahadi's Middle Eastern Market on Atlantic Avenue in Brooklyn, New York or through their website: www.sahadi.com. Perhaps local Middle Eastern markets offer the same choice.

To save time, the apricots may be soaked for a few hours to plump before cooking. The refrigerated jelly stays fresh for months.

Besides jelly, Syrians also enjoy a tasty apricot paste in the form of a leathery sheet. It was considered a treat whenever we shopped downtown Brooklyn as kids. It is available in Middle Eastern stores and some high-end supermarkets. We called it "shoe leather" probably because *Giddo* Richard and his brothers owned a shoe manufacturing business and apricot paste resembled the leather used in their production line.

Ca'ak (page 37), a breakfast cookie, is often topped with apricot jelly and served with Syrian cheese and melon.

3 pounds dried apricots, coarsely chopped (use a food processor)
3/4 cup sugar
Cold water

Put the apricots and sugar into a deep, heavy pot. Add water to cover fruit by 1 inch. Mix and bring to a slow boil uncovered. Lower heat and simmer 40 minutes while occasionally stirring. Add water as needed. Consistency should be slightly thick. When the apricots seem soft, turn off the heat and set aside to cool. Spoon into jars or plastic containers. Cover, refrigerate and enjoy!

BREAKFAST BREAD FLAVORED WITH BLACK CHERRY SEED

Arras *Yield: 24*

This tasty breakfast treat goes well with *mamuneh'ya*, homemade apricot jelly, melon, and a variety of Syrian cheeses. *Mahlab* (powdered black cherry seed) gives it its distinct taste. Kids and adults alike love it!

Another version with dates is sweeter and we recommend serving it without a topping. It can also be served with Syrian cheese and olives on the side. Both breads can be frozen. When ready to use, thaw and heat in a toaster or regular oven at 350 degrees for a few minutes until warm.

If you prepare the full recipe, a heavy-duty mixer, with at least a 4 to 5-quart bowl, must be used. If you do not have a large bowl, it will be necessary to halve the recipe and prepare two batches in a food processor, but it must have a strong motor. Of course you can mix the dough by hand but knead well for at least 5 minutes. The dough will be moist and slightly sticky.

Do not grease the baking pans.

Plain Arras

2 packets active dry yeast
¼ cup warm water
6 cups semolina
3 cups all-purpose flour
1 tablespoon baking powder
2 tablespoons sugar
4 tablespoons mahlab (powder consistency)
¼ teaspoon salt
1 quart whole milk, at room temperature
1 pound (4 sticks) salted butter, melted

Utensils

Design tools (there are specific ones for edges and tops). If you do not have Middle Eastern tools for this purpose, use the bottom of an 8-ounce glass to make an indentation on the top and design the edges with fork tines.

Step 1:

Dissolve yeast in warm water and set aside. Pour the semolina, flour, baking powder, sugar, *mahlab*, and salt into a bowl and blend.

Step 2:

Pour the milk and butter over the dry ingredients and mix on low speed. Add the yeast and water mixture and continue mixing for at least 10 minutes.

Put the dough into a larger bowl; cover with a heavy cloth or towel and set aside in a warm place for 2 hours.

Step 3:

Take a large meatball-size piece of dough and roll in the palms of your hands. If the dough is too sticky, dust your hands with flour when rolling. Place 3 inches apart on ungreased baking trays.

Step 4:

Cover with the same cloth and set aside for another hour. Then roll the design tool around the edge of each *arras* and design the top. Press down when doing this. Cover again and set aside an additional hour before baking.

Step 5:

Preheat oven to 350 degrees. Bake until golden brown on top and bottom; approximately 30 minutes.

Date Arras on following page

Date Arras

Yield: 30

Use the same dough ingredients listed above for Plain Arras with the addition of:

2 (13-ounce) packages pitted pressed dates
2 teaspoons salted butter, softened
6 teaspoons rose water

Follow steps 1, 2, and 3 for plain *arras*, but divide the dough into 30 portions. Mix the dates well with the butter and rose water and set aside. Separate the dates into 30 flattened, oval-shape pieces. Flatten each piece of dough and place one piece of date mixture on it ½ inch in from the edge. Fold over the top half of the dough enclosing the date mixture, and press the edges together. Complete the rising and baking as indicated in steps 4 and 5 for plain arras, though this version may take slightly longer to bake.

BREAKFAST COOKIE

Ca'ak *Yield: 8 to 9 dozen*

Basically, there are two versions of ca'ak, each with its own distinct flavor. Both are excellent and taste wonderful right from the oven. The flavor actually improves over time. Serve at breakfast with string cheese and olives and they are delicious with coffee, especially the Turkish or Arab variety. The cookie can also be served with a topping of homemade apricot jelly (page 33).

You can substitute equal amounts of reserved juices from homemade string cheese for the water indicated.

Follow the same directions for both versions.

Seasoned Ca'ak

1 packet yeast
1¼ cups warm water
1 teaspoon sugar
2 cups semolina
1½ cups (3 sticks) salted butter, melted
4 cups all-purpose flour
1½ teaspoons baking powder
1 tablespoon mahlab (powder consistency)
1 tablespoon anise
1 tablespoon fennel seed
½ tablespoon black caraway seeds (optional)

Plain Ca'ak

1 packet yeast
1¼ cups warm water
2 cups semolina
1½ cups (3 sticks) salted butter, melted
4 cups all-purpose flour
3 tablespoons mahlab (powder consistency)

Step 1:

Mix yeast and warm water (add sugar for seasoned). Set aside. Put the remainder of the ingredients into a heavy-duty mixer and blend. Add the yeast mixture and mix well. Leave the dough in the same bowl, cover with a cloth or towel and keep in a warm place for 1 hour.

Step 2:

Preheat the oven to 350 degrees.

Step 3:

Take a small piece of dough and roll into a ball approximately 1¼ inches in diameter. Make about 15 balls at a time and keep the rest of the dough covered so it doesn't dry out. Roll each ball into finger shapes about 4-inches long. Bend into a circle overlapping the two ends and pinch them together. Place ½-inch apart on an ungreased cookie sheet. Bake for 40 minutes or until golden brown on top and bottom. When the cookies are done, turn the oven off. Pile all the *ca'ak* on one tray and put back in the oven for 1 hour to crisp.

Syrian cheese, ca'ak and apricot jelly

CHEESE

Jib'neh *Yield: 5 braided cheese*

There are two types of Syrian cheese, "block" and "string." They are equally popular and can be purchased at many markets. They can be homemade as well. *Jib'neh* can be served at breakfast with *ca'ak*, and apricot jelly; with olives, melon and/or *mamuneh'ya*; as an appetizer; in pita for lunch with garlic pickles and/or kirby cucumbers; or alone.

The "string" cheese is also known as *Halabi* cheese (*Halabi* meaning Aleppian) and Armenian rope cheese. Virtually all-commercial brands are edible, but vary in appeal depending on the amount of salt and number of caraway seeds preferred. You can make 5 pounds of string cheese for the price of 1 pound store-bought.

Juice will be left over after making string cheese. It can be reserved, refrigerated, and substituted for the water used in preparing *ca'ak* (page 37). Do not leave the cheese uncovered and exposed to the air. It will dry out.

A great idea for lunch or snack is to place a few slices of either cheese into a pita and toasting or heating it until crisp. While still warm, flatten with your hand. If the bread is too hot, place a paper towel over the bread and cover with a potholder before pressing down. We all love the cheese prepared this way.

Block Cheese

1 gallon whole milk
1 rennet tablet, crushed
Kosher salt

Pour the milk into a deep pot and cook at medium heat until warm. Stir in the rennet tablet, mixing often until the cream separates from the milk (15 to 20 minutes). Then, use a large slotted spoon to scoop out the chunks of cheese, placing them into a small metal or plastic basket with openings. Press down lightly to mold the cheese and remove excess, but not all, the liquid. This will keep it moist. Let rest for 15 minutes then turn out onto a plate. Lightly sprinkle kosher salt all over it, pressing the salt into the cheese. If it tastes too salty, simply rinse off. It is better to refrigerate for at least a few hours before slicing.

String Cheese

The sweet cheese can be purchased fresh in bulk form or as prepared mozzarella cheese, unsalted and uncooked from most Middle Eastern markets.

1 gallon cold water
3 tablespoons kosher salt
5 pounds sweet bulk cheese, diced and set aside
2 teaspoons mahlab (powder consistency)
1 teaspoon black caraway seeds

Step 1:

Pour water into a deep pot, add the salt, and stir until it dissolves. Place an egg into the water adding salt until a quarter-size portion of it floats. Set water aside. Use the egg for another purpose.

Step 2:

Place 1 pound cheese on a microwave dish. Place in the microwave for approximately 50 seconds. Remove and test for softness. The pieces should be melted together without being liquefied. If unequally melted, rearrange the cheese on the dish and return to the oven for 10 seconds longer. Remove from the oven and working with your hands, mold the cheese into a smooth ball. Reserve the liquid for later use to prepare *ca'ak* (page 37). Place into a wide shallow bowl. Season with a pinch or two of *mahlab* and caraway seeds. Turn the cheese repeatedly until the *mahlab* and seeds are mixed in well. Repeat the procedure until all the cheese is used.

Step 3:

Roll each ball on top of paper towels to remove excess liquid.

Step 4:

Put your thumbs through the center of the ball and begin stretching it approximately two feet. Rotate the cheese through your hands until firm and smooth. Fold over three times, twist and pull gently and then tuck one end into the other to hold its shape. Soak in the salt water a few hours. Remove, wrap tightly in plastic wrap and refrigerate or freeze.

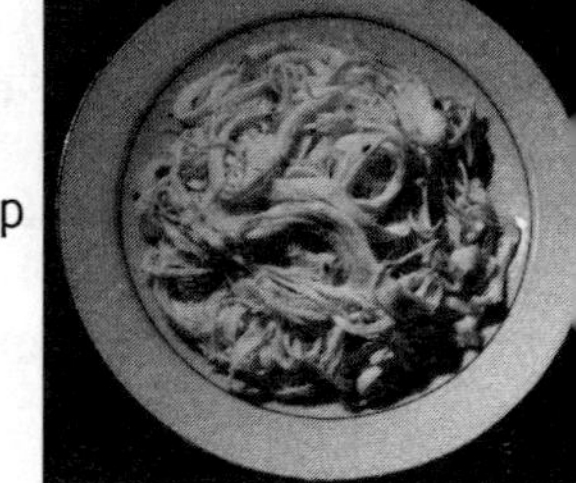

To serve, unravel the braid and separate into thin strings.

SEASONED FLAT BREAD

Za'atar Bread *Yield: 10 pieces*

Za'atar (the spice) can be purchased from many Middle Eastern markets but the quality and taste vary. The same is true of the bread. Preparation for homemade bread is simple and well worth the effort. This bread is great for breakfast or lunch served with olives and any type of Syrian cheese. Freshly baked *za'atar* bread is sold in almost all Middle Eastern bakeries. It tastes best fresh from the oven.

If using frozen dough, Philip has a trick for thawing it quickly. He sprinkles some flour into a large plastic bag, coats the frozen dough lightly with oil, and puts it into the bag. He then places the bag in the center of a pizza tray and places it in an oven with just the pilot flame on. It thaws in approximately 2 hours. He then rubs some flour in the palms of his hands and spreads the dough out. He also puts a little oregano in for a kick!

1½ pounds pizza dough
Olive oil
Za'atar

Utensil
One (14-inch) pizza pan

Step 1:
Preheat oven to 400 degrees.

Step 2:
Oil the pan lightly.

Step 3:
Spread out the dough on the pan. (If using leftover dough from meat and spinach pies, rub lightly with olive oil before spreading out.) With your hand or paper towel, spread a thin layer of oil on top of the dough. Sprinkle the *za'atar* spice generously over the top and drizzle additional oil over the seasoned dough. Bake for 25 minutes or until the crust is lightly browned. Cut into triangles and serve hot.

SEMOLINA PORRIDGE

Mamuneh'ya *Yield: 10 small servings*

On a cold winter morning, a *mamuneh'ya* breakfast will certainly warm you up. Children especially love the flavor and texture of this sweet porridge. Serve alone sprinkled with cinnamon or accompanied by pita, Syrian cheese, *ca'ak*, and melon.

If any *mamuneh'ya* is left over, refrigerate and reheat before serving. Just add a little milk, mix well, and microwave until hot.

¾ cup (1½ sticks) salted butter
1 cup semolina
4½ cups cold water
1 cup sugar
Cinnamon

Step 1:
Melt 1 stick of butter in a medium-size pot (large enough to eventually hold the semolina, water and sugar). Add the semolina and sauté over medium/low heat stirring constantly, until golden brown (approximately 15 minutes). Remove the pot from the stove and cover.

Step 2:
While browning the semolina, mix the water and sugar in another pot and bring to a boil. To avoid a hot splatter on hands, place the pot with the semolina in the sink. Pour the mixture over the semolina and combine. Add the remaining butter and mix well. Cover and set aside for approximately 5 minutes. Mix again and serve in individual dishes, topped with cinnamon.

YOGURT MINT SPREAD

Lebaneh *Yield: Approximately 2 cups*

Though normally eaten at breakfast, *lebaneh* has suddenly become a popular appetizer at sophisticated New York parties. There are excellent commercial brands that can be purchased in any Middle Eastern market. It is rich in calcium and is lactose free.

1 (32-ounce) container plain yogurt (commercial or homemade). Leave in the refrigerator two weeks before using so a "tang" develops.

Garnish
Olive oil
Dried mint

Utensil
Cheesecloth or strainer

Pour the yogurt into cheesecloth or a paper towel lined strainer with medium-size openings. Drip until relatively dry (3 hours). If it is put into cheesecloth, squeeze dry when finished. If it is put into a strainer, push down with a large spoon to remove the excess water. Texture should be creamy. When serving, put the *lebaneh* into a dish or bowl; mix in some dried mint and oil to taste, and sprinkle the top lightly with the oil mixture.

Appetizers

(Mezze)

CHICKPEA DIP

Hummus bil Tahini *Yield: 3 cups*

A ubiquitous and inviting dip, *hummus* is sold not only in all Middle Eastern markets but in many American supermarkets as well. The recipe below is as authentic as possible and our family and guests just love it this way!

Hummus is served mainly as an appetizer but can also be used as a condiment in many different types of pita sandwiches. When presented as an appetizer, garnish with parsley and/or a few sprinkles of cumin and oil. If serving on a flat dish, swirl designs on top with a spoon and pour olive oil into the depressions. It is scrumptious scooped up with pita or pita chips (page 184). In Syria, *hummus* is flooded with olive oil.

Originally, *hummus* was prepared by simmering the chickpeas in their liquid, then draining and reserving it. The chickpeas would be skinned, then placed with the seasonings into a blender and puréed. The reserved liquid was used to thin the purée if required.

We finally discovered that a processor works wonders and you no longer have to boil the chickpeas or remove the skin. This makes it much easier to prepare.

Hummus can be frozen. After thawing, mix until smooth and sprinkle a bit of olive oil, cumin, and/or parsley on top before serving.

Recipe and ingredients on following page

3 medium cloves garlic
2 (15-ounce) cans chickpeas
4 tablespoons sesame paste (tahini)
3 tablespoons fresh lemon juice
2 tablespoons olive oil
1 tablespoon cumin
½ teaspoon kosher salt

Garnish

2 tablespoons chopped flat-leaf parsley

Step 1:

Put the garlic into a food processor and chop fine.

Step 2:

Put 1 can of chickpeas with its liquid into the processor. Strain the chickpeas from the other can, discard the liquid, and add to the processor. Add the tahini, lemon juice, oil, cumin, salt, and blend until smooth.

Proportions can be changed according to individual taste. *Hummus* should be slightly thick. If too thick, add lemon juice.

COLD VINEGARED LAMB ROLL WITH PISTACHIO

Martadala *Yield: approximately 60 slices*

Sitto Alice's grandson, Justin, discovered his love of Syrian food eating *martadala*, his favorite dish, in pita stuffed with stretch (*Halabi*) cheese. itto Helen's children add mayonnaise to the sandwich.

his is a great appetizer on crackers or in pita (mini-pitas are perfect) with liced tomato and lettuce. *Martadala*, sliced and garnished with parsley, is ssential to any *mezze* tray.

he *hubra* should be prepared the day before cooking. Add 1 teaspoon of osher salt to the meat, mix well, and refrigerate.

ime the loaves from the moment they are placed into the boiling inegar/water mixture. If you overcook, the meat will be dry. *Martadala* looks nd tastes best when slightly pink inside.

*2 pounds very lean ground lamb (*hubra*)*
½ cup pistachio nuts, skins removed
½ cup pine nuts
1 large clove garlic, cut into slivers
2 teaspoons da'ah (page 19)
1 tablespoon plus teaspoon kosher salt
¾ cup cold water
3½ cups white vinegar
2 to 3 cloves garlic, minced
5 bay leaves, crumbled

tep 1:

Divide the meat in half and refrigerate one portion. For ease of rolling, put the meat on a sheet of waxed paper or a flat clean surface. Spread the meat out with your hands into an oval shape, ½-inch thick; 4-inches wide and 8-inches long. Keep wetting your hands while you are doing this so the meat does not stick to them.

If smaller loaves are preferred, adjust ingredients and cooking time accordingly.

Step 2:

Divide the pistachio and pine nuts, slivered garlic, *da'ah*, and 1 teaspoon kosher salt in half and set aside one portion. Sprinkle salt and *da'ah* over the meat and press in the pistachios, pine nuts, and garlic approximately ⅛-inch apart, alternating the garlic and nuts. Roll the meat jellyroll fashion and close the ends. Wet your hands with cold water and smooth out the loaf making sure there are no openings. Roll the loaf back and forth until it is completely closed. Place on a dish and put into the refrigerator. Repeat the same procedure for the second portion and refrigerate both loaves for approximately 6 hours or overnight to firm.

Step 3:

Pour the water and vinegar into a wide, deep pot (wide enough to hold the rolls). Add the minced garlic, bay leaves, and 1 tablespoon kosher salt. Stir and bring to a boil. Place the meat into the pot and bring to a second boil. Lower the heat; cover tightly and simmer 10 minutes. Turn over and simmer an additional 11 minutes.

Remove the meat from the water and cool completely before slicing approximately ¼-inch thick. The rolls slice best with a sharp, non-serrated knife.

CURED LAMB

Adeed *Yield: Each piece makes 4 to 5 sandwiches or serves 6 to 8 as an appetizer with cheese and/or olives.*

This is a mouth watering, spicy appetizer or luncheon dish—a Syrian pastrami, if you will. Serve thinly sliced and piled high on a serving dish. Eat with your fingers or around a breadstick, on pita or crackers with Syrian ıeese and olives, or as a pita sandwich. Commercially known as *bastrami*, *deed* can also be purchased at Middle Eastern markets.

ıis dish needs to cure several days outdoors in freezing weather.

12 to 14 lamb fillets, approximately ¾ pound each (filet mignon may be substituted)
Kosher salt
¼ pound dried fenugreek
2 tablespoons cumin
2 tablespoons paprika
1 tablespoon ground red pepper
10 cloves garlic, crushed
1 cup cold water

Utensils

One 1½-inch diameter pole, 3 to 4 feet long
Heavy thread or thin rope

ep 1:

Make a hole near the edge of each fillet and run a section of heavy thread or rope through it. Tie the ends together to form a loop large enough to slide over the pole. Salt the meat heavily on both sides, pressing it into the meat. Put the meat in a deep platter or in a pan and refrigerate for 24 hours. Remove the meat and, holding the pole horizontally, hang the meat from it. Cover completely with cheesecloth for protection from animals. To begin the curing process, hang the pole outdoors in below freezing temperature for two days. The blood will drip from the meat.

ontinued

Step 2:

Remove the cheesecloth and meat from the pole; put meat into a deep pan and wipe off the excess salt and blood with paper towels. Do not remove all the salt. Press down on the meat with your fingers or roll lightly with a rolling pin to keep the remaining salt in the meat.

Step 3:

Put the fenugreek, cumin, paprika, red pepper, and garlic into a bowl and mix. Add the water and mix until pasty, but not too thick, adding additional water as needed. Cover the meat completely with the paste. Place in the refrigerator for 24 hours then hang outdoors again covered with cheesecloth. This process may take 2 to 3 days to cure. When complete dry, the meat will be dark brown/reddish in color. Wrap each piece and refrigerate or slice thin and serve. If you have an electric slicer, by all means use it, and slice as thin as possible. A single piece should last a few weeks in the refrigerator, if it has not been eaten before then. It may be frozen for later use.

EGGPLANT DIP

Baba Ghanouj *Yield: 3 cups*

B*aba ghanouj* is as popular as *hummus* and is sold in many American supermarkets. It is a must at *sah'rhas* or family parties. Serve garnished with rsley and/or lemon wedges, placing pita and/or crackers on the side. For a ıcier presentation, add some pomegranate seeds. You can also make crevices lines in this dip with a spoon and pour oil into them.

3 pounds eggplant (black skinned; light density)
2 tablespoons sesame paste (tahini)
1 teaspoon kosher salt
2 large cloves garlic, mashed
¼ cup fresh lemon juice
2½ tablespoons olive oil

ep 1:
Wipe the skin of the eggplants with a damp paper towel and place on a baking tray. Pierce them in a few places with a fork and put into the broiler. Turn over. The eggplant will eventually collapse. Once the fork easily penetrates the entire eggplant and the inside feels soft, remove the pan from the oven. This procedure may take 30 minutes.

ep 2:
Cut off the ends of each eggplant and split down the center. Scoop out contents, discarding the skin. Remove as many seeds as possible. Mash the innards in a bowl or use a processor to purée. Texture should be slightly lumpy. Add the *tahini*, salt, garlic, lemon juice, and oil to the eggplant and continue mixing. Taste and adjust seasonings accordingly.

GRAPE LEAVES FILLED WITH VEGETABLES AND RICE

Yebrat Syamee *Yield: Approximately 70*

This is a wonderful Lenten meal. *Yebrat syamee* can be served as an app tizer or at a luncheon/buffet with yogurt on the side. Stack them in a ser ing dish and garnish with lemon wedges.

2½ cups chopped flat-leaf parsley
2 cups chopped fresh tomatoes
2 large yellow onions, minced and squeezed tightly to remove excess water
1 large green or red bell pepper, minced
½ cup walnuts, chopped medium/fine
¼ cup pine nuts
1 (15.5-ounce) can chickpeas, drained
1 cup uncooked white rice
1¼ tablespoons kosher salt
1½ tablespoons allspice
½ pound grape leaves or more as needed (see Bas Guidelines page 29 for leaf preparation)*
1 cup olive oil
1 cup cold water
1 cup fresh or bottled lemon juice

Step 1:
Mix in a bowl the parsley, tomatoes, onions, pepper, walnuts, pine nuts, chickpeas, rice, salt, and allspice. Periodically mix while stuffing the leave

Step 2:
Place a grape leaf on a flat surface and put 1 tablespoon of stuffing widt wise across the widest part. Fold the sides over the ends of the stuffing and roll gently but tightly until sealed. Do not use too much stuffing, it may cause the leaf to rip.

Step 3:

Place the grape leaves into a wide, deep pot over a steamer basket. Pour the oil over the leaves followed by the water and lemon juice. Place an inverted plate over the leaves to prevent shifting. Cover the pot tightly; bring to a boil; lower the heat and simmer 35 minutes or until the rice and leaves are tender. Close the heat; remove the cover and let stand until cool. Serve at room temperature.

*Baby eggplants can be substituted for grape leaves (*bantanjan syamee*). Use 14 eggplants, and cook approximately 10 minutes longer or until the vegetables and rice are tender. Let stand until cool and serve at room temperature. Also wonderful as a luncheon/buffet choice with yogurt on the side!

For eggplant preparation, see *bantenjan mahshee*, page 122.

How to roll grape leaves

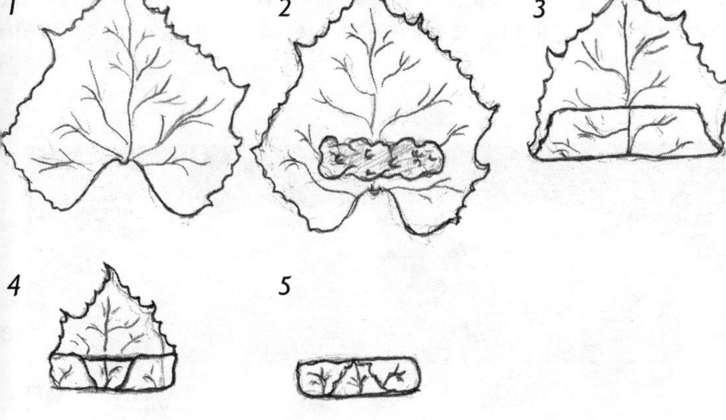

LAMB TARTARE

Kibbeh Nayeh — *Yield: 8 to 10 servings*

Primarily served nowadays as an appetizer, *kibbeh nayeh*, the lamb versio of beef tartare, can also be served as a main dish. For years, our familie served *kibbeh nayeh* with meat *yebrat* as an entrée. This combination makes fo a great Sunday lunch. This is the quintessential Syrian/Lebanese meal no found elsewhere in the Arab world, save Jordan, and is the basis for man other popular *kibbeh* dishes.

For an attractive presentation, place the meat onto a small platter and smoot out with a wet hand to a preferred thickness and shape, removing wrinkle Use fork tines to create a design on the surface of the meat. Garnish with pars ley or mint and/or a sprinkle of allspice. For a fancier effect, top with pom granate seeds or place a few stalks of scallions on the edge of the serving pla ter. Serve with raw onion wedges immersed in a bowl of cold water on the sid

To eat, flatten your portion with a fork and sprinkle a little olive oil over i Scoop with pita right off your plate or eat with a fork (very American). If the is some *kibbeh* left over, it can be used to make *kibbeh asieck* (page 106) *kibbeh ba'id* (page 99).

½ teaspoon kosher salt
*1 pound very lean ground lamb (*hubra*)*
¾ cup #1 wheat
1 medium yellow onion, grated

Step 1:
Add the salt to the meat and mix well. Refrigerate until use.

Step 2:
Place the wheat into a bowl and cover with cold water. Drain through a fine strainer; rinse again; drain and refrigerate for ½ hour before using.

Step 3:
Put the grated onion into the bowl containing the wheat. Add the meat and knead well, wetting your hands in cold water occasionally while mixing until you have a somewhat firm, smooth texture, and pleasing flavor. Taste and add additional salt and/or water if needed. There is a ratio that is learned from experience.

OLIVES

Zatoon

As a finger food, olives are a must on any Middle Eastern table whether at home or in a restaurant. At parties, they are always a part of a *mezze* tray. Ideally, use olives fresh from the barrel. Drain; rinse in cold water and add olive oil and lemon juice for a tangy taste. Mix well.

Italian bread or pita dipped into the liquid is delicious. Often, the bottled olives from a supermarket are as good as those stored in a barrel. The prices are the same in the Middle Eastern stores. We prefer kalamata and alphonso olives and feel they are both equally popular and tasty. Generally Middle Eastern merchants have barrels of olives and offer you a free taste. The quality and type of olive differ by store, but it is a treat to get a nibble.

Olives are a basic part of any *mezze* presentation.

PICKLED CUCUMBERS

Khyard Makboos *Yield: approximately 15 pickles*

These cucumbers will last a week or two in the refrigerator if they are not devoured before then. They are garlicky and tangy, just the way we like them!

3 pounds small kirby cucumbers
⅔ cup white vinegar
1 tablespoon kosher salt
4 cloves garlic, minced
2 tablespoons coriander

Utensil
2-quart jar

Step 1:
Wash and scrub the cucumbers thoroughly. Place them one at a time vertically in the jar making sure they fit tightly together. Pour in the vinegar and add cold water until the jar is filled. Hold the cucumbers in the jar with your hand and pour the water and vinegar mixture out into a small pot. Set the jar aside.

Step 2:
Add the salt to the water and vinegar mixture and bring to a boil. Remove the pot and set aside to cool.

Step 3:
Mix the garlic with the coriander and put on top of the cucumbers in the jar. Then pour the water and vinegar mixture over them. Place a piece of waxed paper over the top of the jar, overlapping the sides. Cover tightly and turn upside down. Leave overnight on a table or counter. The next morning, turn upright but **do not open** for three days. Refrigerate and serve cold.

PICKLED TURNIPS

Liffit Makboos *Yield: 10 to 12*

Pickled turnips are just as good and tangy as the cucumber pickles.

3 pounds fresh turnips
1 fresh, small beet, peeled and diced
¾ cup white vinegar
4 tablespoons kosher salt

Utensil
2-quart jar

Step 1:
Peel and rinse the turnips and trim off the stems. Cut into small chunks. Put in a bowl; cover with cold water and set aside for a few hours. Drain; rinse and repeat the procedure. This will remove the bitter taste.

Step 2:
Place half the turnips into the jar. Add the beet pieces and place the remainder of the turnips on top. Add the vinegar and salt and fill the jar with cold water. Place a piece of waxed paper over the top of the jar, overlapping the sides. Cover tightly and turn upside down. Leave overnight on a table or counter. The next morning turn upright but **do not open** for three days. Refrigerate and serve cold.

RED PEPPER DIP

M'hammara — *Yield: 3 to 4 cups*

This well-liked dip can be made as spicy hot as you like; just add more red pepper. Our *Sittos'* recipe has a coarse texture, but many prefer it as a thick paste and serve as a spread. *M'hammara* has a distinct taste and is always a welcome treat at parties. The red peppers can be prepared beforehand and frozen for later use. Sprinkle with olive oil, do not mix, and then freeze.

For an appetizing presentation, garnish with pomegranate seeds and parsley or lemon wedges and serve with crackers, pita or toasted pita chips (page 184). Any leftovers can be frozen; thaw and mix well before serving.

2 pounds fresh red bell peppers
3 (6-inch) pitas, toasted crisp or 6 zwieback crackers
2 cups shelled walnuts, chopped medium/fine
1 teaspoon ground red pepper (cayenne)
1½ teaspoons kosher salt
½ cup olive oil
¼ cup fresh lemon juice
½ cup pomegranate molasses (page 185)

Step 1:

Rinse the peppers; cut in half and remove the seeds. Pat dry and dice. Use a food processor to chop medium/fine. Cut the peppers into quarters to maintain consistency before chopping. Put into a colander to drain, then place into a bowl. Set aside.

Step 2:

Break pita or crackers into pieces; put into a food processor and chop medium/fine. Put the bread or crackers and walnuts into the bowl with the peppers and mix well by hand. Add the red pepper, salt, oil, lemon juice, and molasses and mix again. If the mixture seems too dry, add more oil; it should be moist. Put into a deep serving dish and top with garnish.

Soups

(Shour'ba)

CHICKEN SOUP

Shour'ba Jaj *Yield: 6 to 7 servings*

Did you ever wish you had a bowl of homemade chicken soup to warm your insides when you were feeling "under the weather"? If so, this is the potage to satisfy your craving. If you prefer the soup tart we recommend adding lemon juice. It can be served as a full meal with crackers or toast and jelly or as a "soup and sandwich" lunch.

If you prefer your soup with less chicken, use the remainder to make a salad or freeze for later use.

1 (3-pound) chicken
1 medium yellow onion, minced
1 cup minced celery
1 cup minced carrots
½ cup uncooked white rice
½ cup lemon juice (optional)
Kosher salt to taste
Pepper to taste
½ teaspoon allspice
1 (8-ounce) can cream of chicken soup

Step 1:
Wash the chicken thoroughly. Place into a large pot and add enough cold water to cover. Bring the water to a boil; lower the heat and remove the scum from the top before adding the onion. Cover with lid tilted and simmer for 1 hour.

Step 2:
Carefully remove the chicken from the pot and set aside. While it is still warm remove the meat from the bones. Discard the skin and other debris; chop the meat into chunks and refrigerate. Pour the broth through a strainer into a bowl and refrigerate until jelled.

Step 3:
Remove excess fat from the top of the broth. Pour the broth into a deep pot and bring to a boil. Lower the heat and add the celery, carrots, rice,

lemon juice (optional), salt, pepper and allspice. Mix, cover with lid tilted, and simmer for 1 hour or until the rice and vegetables are cooked. Add the cream of chicken soup, chicken pieces, and mix well. Simmer an additional 20 minutes.

Note: An option to consider is Philip's "leftover" chicken soup. He uses left over meat and bones from a store-bought rotisserie chicken. Remove chicken from the bones and set aside. Put the bones and two chicken bouillon cubes into 8 cups of cold water and bring to a boil. Lower the heat, cover with lid tilted, and simmer 30 minutes. Remove bones. Add the rice, spices, lemon juice, vegetables, and simmer an additional 20 minutes. Add the chicken and simmer 15 minutes longer. The taste of the rotisserie chicken adds wonderful flavor to the soup and the lemon juice is his key ingredient.

LENTIL, RICE, AND WHEAT SOUP

Makhlootha *Yield: 6 servings*

This uniquely flavored soup is a meal in itself. Add toasted pieces of pita, pita chips (page 184) or croutons and serve with a Syrian salad.

½ cup orange lentils
7½ cups cold water
¼ cup uncooked white rice
¼ cup #4 wheat
2 teaspoons kosher salt
2 medium yellow onions, diced
¼ cup olive oil
3 cloves garlic, minced
1½ tablespoons cumin
1 tablespoon coriander
¼ teaspoon saffron or turmeric (optional)

ep 1:
Check the lentils for small stones; if any discard. Rinse and place into a deep pot. Add the water, rice, wheat, and salt. Bring to a boil and after a few minutes add 1 diced onion. Lower the heat, cover with lid tilted, and simmer for 1 hour.

ep 2:
Approximately ½ hour after the lentils begin cooking, pour the oil into a skillet and heat. Add the remaining onion and the garlic. Sauté until lightly browned (this should take at least 20 minutes) then pour over the soup. Mix well. Cover with lid tilted; stir occasionally, and cook an additional hour. Soup will be thick and creamy. If you feel it is too thick, add water.

ep 3:
When the soup is cooked, add the cumin, coriander, and saffron or turmeric if desired. Mix well.

LENTIL, SPINACH AND NOODLE SOUP

Rhisthaya *Yield: 4 to 6 servings*

We guarantee you will enjoy this aromatic soup. For variety, dried mir (*nah'nah*) may be substituted for spinach.

1 cup dark lentils
12 cups cold water
2 large yellow onions, diced
Kosher salt to taste
2 tablespoons coriander
2 carrots, chopped (optional)
1 (10-ounce) package fresh spinach, stems removed and broken into medium-size pieces or ½ cup dried mint
3 cloves garlic, minced
¼ cup olive oil
½ pound narrow egg noodles or ditalini noodles

Step 1:

Check the lentils for small stones; if any discard. Rinse and place into a deep pot. Add the water and bring to a boil. Add half the onions, salt, and coriander. Lower the heat, cover with lid tilted, and simmer for 20 minutes. Add the carrots if using and simmer an additional 10 minutes. Add the spinach or mint and cook 5 minutes longer or until the vegetables are fully cooked. Add the noodles, and cook per package directions, no longer.

Step 2:

As the soup begins to boil, sauté the remaining onion and garlic in the c for 15 minutes or until nicely browned. Mix occasionally. Pour over the soup, mix and continue cooking.

YOGURT AND LAMB MEATBALL SOUP

Kibbeh Lebanneya *Yield: 8 servings*

This wholesome winter soup is quite unusual. Made from yogurt, it is rich in calcium and soothing to the palette. *Kibbeh lebanneya's* distinct flavor omes from the cooked rice and butter cinnamon stuffed meatballs. The Jerro ;randchildren and Philip's niece Michele favor this meal.

erve hot in individual soup bowls with raw vegetables and pita on the side. \ tasty side dish is a vinegar-soaked red onion. Just quarter the onion and oak in white vinegar for an hour in the refrigerator.

'he meatballs can be prepared, boiled, and frozen for later use.

1 teaspoon kosher salt
*2 pounds very lean ground lamb (*hubra*)*
1½ cups #1 wheat
1 large yellow onion, grated
¾ cup (1½ sticks) salted butter, cold
Allspice
Cinnamon
1 cup uncooked white rice
1 teaspoon corn starch
3 quarts whole milk yogurt, preferably homemade (see page 191)

tep 1:
Add the salt to the meat and mix well. Refrigerate.

tep 2:
Put the wheat into a bowl and cover with cold water. Drain into a fine strainer; rinse again; drain and refrigerate for ½ hour.

tep 3:
Put the grated onion into the bowl containing the wheat. Add the meat and knead well, wetting your hands in cold water occasionally while mixing

until you have a somewhat firm, smooth texture and pleasing flavor. Taste and add additional salt and/or water if needed.

Step 4:

Cut the butter into bits (chickpea size, approximately 100). Halve the portion and put on two dishes. Sprinkle generously with allspice and cinnamon until completely covered. Since butter softens quickly, we suggest putting one dish into the freezer while stuffing the meatballs. It is easier to handle the butter when ice cold.

Take a small piece of meat (*kibbeh*) and roll into a ball 1¼ inches in diameter. Make a hole with your thumb and twist around until the opening is large enough to hold a piece of butter. Insert the butter and close the top. Sitto Helen recommends keeping a small bowl of ice water nearby so you can wet your hands while smoothing out the *kibbeh* balls. Make sure they are completely closed and smooth. You will have to roll them around in your hand quite a few times in order to do this. Cover the *kibbeh* balls and place in the refrigerator for a few hours or overnight before boiling.

Step 5:

Fill a large pot with lightly salted water and bring to a boil. Gradually place the *kibbeh* balls into the water and once they rise to the top lower the heat. Simmer 3 minutes. Do not cover the pot. Pour into a colander and set aside.

Step 6:

Bring 2½ cups cold, lightly salted water to a boil and add the rice. Stir and cover the pot tightly. Simmer 20 minutes or until the rice is tender. The rice should be slightly moist. Set aside.

Step 7:

Put the cornstarch into a 6 to 8-quart pot; add the yogurt and mix. Turn the heat on medium/low. Stir gently for approximately 40 minutes. Stir in the cooked rice. Lower the heat and simmer ½ hour. Do not cover. Stir occasionally. Add the *kibbeh* balls and simmer an additional hour or until they are heated through.

Note: Sitto Alice cooked the raw rice in the yogurt mixture. Strain the yogurt into a pot, and mix in 1 cup of rice. Add 3 cups of slightly salted water and bring to a slow boil. Simmer, stirring constantly and gently on medium/low heat until the rice is cooked. Put the raw *kibbeh* balls into the yogurt mixture and cook for approximately 15 minutes on very low heat until cooked through. Leave pot uncovered throughout process.

Salads

(Salata)

AUNT MARY'S POTATO SALAD

Bata'ta Salata *Yield: 8 to 10 servings*

Most everyone loves potato salad and has his/her own best recipe. Try this family recipe for a surprising change. A more traditional Syrian potato salad is presented on page 88.

3 pounds red potatoes
1 medium yellow onion, grated and squeezed to remove excess juices
¾ cup chopped celery
1 cup mayonnaise
½ cup whole milk
¼ cup white vinegar
¼ cup fresh lemon juice
1 teaspoon sugar
1 teaspoon kosher salt
½ teaspoon allspice

Step 1:

Scrub the potatoes and rinse well. Put them into a deep pot; cover with cold water and bring to a boil. Cover with lid tilted; lower the heat and slow boil for approximately 30 minutes. Pierce each potato with a fork to test doneness and remove when cooked. Depending on the size of the potatoes, cooking time will vary, so adjust accordingly. Drain potatoes in a colander. Cool, peel, cut into cubes, place in a bowl and set aside. Avoid overcooking.

Step 2:

Mix the onion, celery, mayonnaise, milk, vinegar, lemon juice, sugar, salt, and allspice in a saucepan. Cook on low heat until the mixture comes to a slow boil. Remove from heat and mix. Pour the dressing over the potatoes and mix gently.

Step 3:

Refrigerate a few hours or overnight. When ready to serve, mix again; taste and add additional condiments if needed.

Consistency should be slightly thick.

COLE SLAW SALAD

Malfouf Salata *Yield: 10 servings*

Malfouf salata tastes completely different from that offered in most delicatessens. Mint and garlic are the key to its distinctiveness and we highly recommend that you try cole slaw this way. The dressing can be prepared beforehand and refrigerated. Consistency should be slightly thick and the taste, slightly tart. The salad tastes better if it is mixed a few hours before serving.

2½ pounds cabbage (firm head)
2 carrots, grated (optional)
½ cup mayonnaise
¼ cup white vinegar
3 tablespoons fresh lemon juice
2 cloves garlic, minced
3 teaspoons dried mint
1 teaspoon kosher salt
½ teaspoon black pepper

Step 1:

Rinse the cabbage and discard the loose leaves. Pat dry and cut into quarters. Place the cabbage flat side down on a cutting board. Slice as thin as possible with a very sharp knife and place into a salad bowl. We do not recommend chopping the cabbage in a food processor. We tried it one time and the results were disappointing. Add the carrots if desired.

Step 2:

Put the mayonnaise, vinegar, lemon juice, garlic, mint, salt, and pepper into a bowl. Mix well and pour over the cabbage. Mix again and serve, or refrigerate for later use.

GREEN BEAN SALAD

Fowleh Salata *Yield: 8 to 10 servings*

Most Syrian salads are wonderful with steaks, chops, *shish kabob*, and any kind of roast or lamb dishes. For a great presentation at a dinner party, garnish with parsley and pomegranate seeds!

2 pounds green beans, stems removed, rinsed, and halved
2 cloves garlic, minced
1 teaspoon allspice
3 tablespoons red or white vinegar
¼ cup olive oil
1 teaspoon kosher salt
1 medium red onion, thinly sliced

Step 1:
Bring a pot of water to a boil. Add the beans; lower the heat and simmer (cover with lid tilted) until tender/crisp, 8 to 10 minutes. Drain in a colander and cool.

Step 2:
Mix the garlic, allspice, vinegar, oil, and salt in a bowl. Pour over the beans. Add the onion; mix and serve.

GREEN SALAD WITH PINE NUTS

Each *Yield: 4 servings as a meal; 8 or more as a side dish*

Our cousin Rita Antaki-Kassis, Aunt Mary's daughter, contributed this recipe. It is one of her family's favorites.

In order to save time, prepare the parsley, lettuce, onions, and peppers the day before and refrigerate.

For leftovers, add additional oil and mix again just before serving.

4 cups chopped flat-leaf parsley
2 large heads romaine lettuce
3 large red or green bell peppers
2 cups #1 wheat
2 medium yellow onions, minced (do not use a processor)

Dressing
1 cup olive oil
½ cup fresh or bottled lemon juice
2¼ cups tomato paste
½ cup pine nuts
1 teaspoon kosher salt

Step 1:
Remove parsley stems. Rinse the leaves well and squeeze tightly before placing on paper towels to dry. Turn periodically to hasten the drying process. Once the parsley is dry, use a food processor to chop medium/fine. Put into a bowl and set aside or refrigerate for later use.

Step 2:
Remove the core from the lettuce and separate the leaves. Rinse well and drain in a colander. Place on paper towels to dry; turning periodically. If using the next day, wrap the lettuce in paper towels; place into a plastic bag and refrigerate.

tep 3:

Rinse the peppers, remove the stems and seeds, pat dry and dice. Set aside or refrigerate for later use.

tep 4:

One hour before serving, rinse the wheat in a bowl and drain through a fine strainer. Return to the bowl and place into the refrigerator for 1/2 hour.

tep 5:

Add the parsley, peppers, and onions to the wheat. Pour the oil and lemon juice over the mixture and add the tomato paste, pine nuts, and salt. Mix well, and refrigerate. The salad should be cold when serving.

tep 6:

Take a lettuce leaf and place a large spoonful of the salad on top. Fold and enjoy! *Each* is eaten sandwich style.

MACARONI SALAD

Macaron'eh Salata *Yield: 6 to 8 servings*

What makes this salad "Syrian" is the allspice (*b'har*). Guests always comment on its unique taste and it is great to say, "this is how our grandparents made it."

½ pound elbow macaroni
½ red bell pepper, minced
1 small yellow onion, grated
½ cup minced celery
½ cup grated carrots
10 black pitted olives, sliced

Dressing
½ cup mayonnaise
¼ cup white vinegar
1 teaspoon kosher salt
½ teaspoon allspice

Step 1:
Boil the macaroni per package directions. Pour into a colander; cool and pour into a bowl. Add the pepper, onion, celery, carrots, and olives.

Step 2:
Put the mayonnaise into a bowl. Add the vinegar, salt, and allspice and mix well. Pour over the macaroni and vegetables. Mix and refrigerate. Before serving, mix again; taste and add additional condiments if needed.

MIXED GREEN SALAD WITH OLIVES

Salata *Yield: 4 servings*

This salad is similar to *fattoush* (page 87) but without the bread. As a personal choice, ingredients can be added or deleted at will as in any of the salads we list. *Salata* is very tasty and goes well with almost any American meal and Syrian lamb dishes.

½ head iceberg or romaine lettuce
1 medium tomato, diced
1 medium cucumber (preferably kirby), diced
1 clove garlic, minced
1 small yellow or red onion, diced
1 tablespoon dried mint
10 alphonso or black olives

Dressing
⅛ cup olive oil
2 tablespoons white vinegar or fresh lemon juice
½ teaspoon kosher salt
1 teaspoon allspice

Step 1:
Remove the core from the lettuce, separate the leaves, rinse, drain well, and cut into small pieces.

Step 2:
Place the lettuce into a salad bowl and add the tomato, cucumber, garlic, onion, mint, and olives.

Step 3:
Pour the oil and vinegar (or lemon juice) into a small bowl; add the salt and allspice and mix well. Pour over the greens. Mix and serve.

MUSHROOM SALAD

Fit'ir Salata *Yield: 6 servings*

For a new take on an old standby, try this recipe, seasoned with garlic ar allspice. You will really appreciate the change!

3 pounds fresh button mushrooms
¼ cup olive oil
4 tablespoons fresh lemon juice
1 clove garlic, minced
½ cup chopped flat-leaf parsley
½ teaspoon allspice
¼ teaspoon kosher salt

Step 1:

Remove and discard ¼ of the stem of each mushroom. Rinse and put them into a pot of boiling water. Lower the heat (do not cover), and sim mer for 5 minutes, **no longer**. Drain in a colander, cool, then put into a deep bowl.

Step 2:

Pour the oil and lemon juice into a bowl. Add the garlic, parsley, allspice salt and mix well. Pour over the mushrooms; mix again and serve.

PARSLEY AND CRACKED WHEAT SALAD

Ta'bouleh *Yield: 6 to 8 servings*

This very popular salad has "gone American." It is sold in many international markets and gourmet shops and goes well with grilled fish or meat.

Ve prefer the salad tart and the amount of lemon juice, oil, and spices is defiitely personal. Michele, Sitto Alice's granddaughter, rightfully discovered hat the key ingredient in making this delicious salad is the mint. When in oubt, add more and if you prefer more wheat or greens, feel free to adjust ccordingly.

or convenience, the salad can be mixed one hour before serving and refrigerted. Fresh mint can also be used. Remove the leaves from the stems; wash he mint thoroughly and dry well before chopping.

½ cup #1 wheat
4½ cups chopped flat-leaf parsley
2 bunches scallions
¼ cup dried mint

Dressing
¼ cup fresh lemon juice
¼ cup olive oil
1 teaspoon kosher salt
1 teaspoon allspice

Garnish
3 large tomatoes, diced
Lemon wedges (optional)

tep 1:
Soak the wheat in cold water for 1 hour or until it softens. Drain well and squeeze tightly to remove excess water. Set aside.

ontinued

Step 2:

Remove the stems from the parsley leaves. Rinse well and squeeze tightl before placing on paper towels to dry. Turn periodically to hasten the drying process; this may take a few hours. Once the parsley is dry, put into food processor and chop medium/fine. Put into a bowl and refrigerate.

Step 3:

Remove the roots from the scallions; rinse well and place on paper towe to dry or pat dry. Chop medium/fine. Put into the bowl with the parsley and set aside.

Step 4:

Add the wheat and mint to the parsley and scallions and mix. Pour the lemon juice and oil over the mixture; add the salt and allspice and mix again until thoroughly blended.

Before serving, arrange on a platter and garnish with the tomatoes and lemon wedges if desired.

PARSLEY, ROMAINE LETTUCE AND CRACKED WHEAT SALAD

Suf'souf *Yield: 10 to 12 servings*

For reasons now lost to history, our family calls *ta'bouleh* *"suf'souf."* Almost all of the ingredients are the same except for the addition of romaine lettuce. Virginia prepares the lettuce, parsley, and scallions a day before serving. She wraps the "greens" in paper towels (to remove excess water); places them into a plastic bag and refrigerates until ready to chop. When chopping the scallions and lettuce for *suf'souf*, do so by hand; do **not** use a processor because the consistency tends to be mushy.

Like *ta'bouleh*, this salad should be tart. Just vary the amount of lemon juice and spices. Fresh mint can also be used instead of dried. Remove the leaves from the stems; wash the mint thoroughly and dry well before chopping.

3 cups chopped flat-leaf parsley
2 medium heads romaine lettuce
2 bunches scallions
1 cup #1 wheat
½ cup dried mint

Dressing
¾ cup olive oil
1 cup fresh lemon juice
2 teaspoons kosher salt

Garnish
3 large tomatoes, diced

Step 1:
Remove the stems from the parsley leaves. Rinse the leaves well and squeeze tightly before placing on paper towels to dry. Turn periodically to speed up the drying process; this may take a few hours. Once the parsley is dry put into a food processor and chop medium/fine. Put into a bowl and refrigerate.

Continued

Step 2:

Remove the core from the lettuce and separate the leaves. Remove the roots from the scallions; rinse the lettuce and scallions well and place or paper towels to dry.

Step 3:

Soak the wheat in cold water for 1 hour or until it softens. Pour into a fine strainer and drain well. Squeeze tightly to remove excess water. Set aside.

Step 4:

Put the lettuce leaves and scallions on a chopping board. Take a few leaves and place some scallions on top. Roll the lettuce around the scallions (easier to chop) and with a very sharp knife chop medium/fine. Repeat the process until all the lettuce and scallions are chopped. Place into a deep bowl. Add the parsley, wheat, mint and mix. Pour the oil an lemon juice over the mixture, add the salt and mix until thoroughly blended.

Garnish with the tomatoes.

PITA BREAD SALAD

Fattoush *Yield: 6 to 8 servings*

This is a popular salad, set off by its garlic-flavored pita chips and mint. *Fattoush* is easy to prepare and goes well with any *kibbeh* dish or entrée. For an extra "kick," garnish with *za'atar*.

1 head romaine or iceberg lettuce
2 teaspoons salted butter, softened
1 large pita
1 teaspoon garlic powder
1 clove garlic, crushed
1 medium kirby cucumber, peeled and diced
1 small red onion, diced
2 teaspoons dried mint or chopped fresh mint
10 alphonso or black olives, pitted
1 medium tomato, diced

Dressing
¼ cup olive oil
3 tablespoons white vinegar or fresh lemon juice
Kosher salt to taste
Black pepper to taste

Step 1:
Remove the core from the lettuce, rinse, drain well, and shred into small pieces.

Step 2:
Butter the pita lightly, sprinkle with garlic powder, toast well, and crush into small pieces. Place the pita, lettuce, garlic, cucumber, onion, mint, olives, and tomato into a salad bowl and toss well.

Step 3:
Combine the oil, vinegar or lemon juice, and salt and pepper in a bowl. Pour over the salad mixture and mix well.

If you prefer your salad tart, add additional vinegar or lemon juice.

SYRIAN POTATO SALAD

Bata'ta Salata *Yield: 8 to 10 servings*

Here is a more traditional Syrian potato salad. The unique flavor comes from the allspice.

3 pounds red potatoes
1/4 cup white vinegar
1/2 cup olive oil
1/2 cup chopped flat-leaf parsley
1 medium yellow onion, minced
2 teaspoons kosher salt
1 teaspoon allspice

Step 1:

Scrub the potatoes and rinse well. Put them into a deep pot; cover with cold water and bring to a boil. Cover with lid tilted; lower the heat and slow boil for approximately 30 minutes. Pierce each potato with a fork to test doneness and remove when cooked. Depending on the size of the potatoes, cooking time will vary, so adjust accordingly. Drain potatoes in a colander. Cool, peel, cut into cubes, place in a bowl, and set aside. Avoid overcooking.

Step 2:

Pour the vinegar and oil into a bowl. Add the parsley, onion, salt, and allspice and mix well. Pour over the potatoes and mix again. Refrigerate a few hours or overnight. When ready to serve, mix again; taste and add additional condiments if needed.

YOGURT SALAD

Leban Salata *Yield: 4 to 5 servings.*

Yogurt is often used as a topping or side dish for many Syrian meals. It can also be prepared as a salad and makes for a fine lunch on a hot summer day. If used as a complement to an entrée, it consists of just yogurt and chopped lettuce leaves and/or cucumbers and a sprinkling of mint. As a luncheon treat by itself, garlic and a touch of salt are added to these other ingredients.

Quantities can be halved or quartered for individual servings and adjusted to personal tastes.

½ head iceberg lettuce, rinsed, drained and shredded
1 cucumber, peeled and diced
1 clove garlic, minced
1 quart yogurt, commercial or homemade (page 191)
1 teaspoon dried mint
Pinch of kosher salt

Step 1:
Put lettuce in a bowl; add cucumber and garlic and mix.

Step 2:
Gently stir in yogurt. Add mint and salt and mix.

Entrées

BAKED EGGPLANT WITH GROUND LAMB TOPPING

Nez'eleh *Yield: 6 to 8 servings*

Nez'eleh consists of slices of eggplant topped with a flavorful blend of sautéed chopped lamb and spices. It can be prepared beforehand, making it a first-rate choice for a luncheon or buffet as well as an entrée.

Fresh diced tomatoes can be added to the meat mixture or placed on top of the prepared eggplant before baking. Sitto Helen does not add tomatoes to the meat mixture but Sitto Alice did. It is a personal choice.

Serve with Syrian rice, and any Syrian salad and pita.

3 pounds or 3 medium eggplants
Kosher salt
Canola oil for frying
Vegetable shortening for frying
*1 pound ground lamb (*kafta*)*
1 medium yellow onion, chopped medium/fine
1 tablespoon da'ah (page 19)
3 tablespoons pine nuts
¼ cup cold water
1 (8-ounce) can tomato sauce or 1 (15-ounce) can diced tomatoes

Step 1:

a) Rinse the unpeeled eggplant and pat dry. Cut off stems and slice eggplant to ½-inch thickness. Salt lightly and place slices on a platter with paper towels between the layers. Press lightly on the paper towels to absorb excess water and salt.

or

b) Rinse the unpeeled eggplant and pat dry. Slice in half lengthwise and again to quarter.* Slit each quarter lengthwise along the ridge being careful not to cut too deeply. Salt lightly and place each piece on a platter with paper towels between the layers. Press lightly on the paper towels to absorb excess water and salt.

*Baby eggplants can also be used; slice in half lengthwise only, making a slit down the center. Proceed accordingly.

Step 2:

In a large frying pan heat the oil and shortening until the shortening melts. For full flavor, the cooking liquid should be at least 1-inch deep, but for "light"* diets, you can use less. Fry the slices until the outer skin is soft and the pulp is tender. Do not overcook. Remove each slice and drain well on paper towels. Set aside.

*To reduce oil absorption, fry the eggplant slices lightly and then microwave until tender.

Step 3:

Sauté the meat in a frying pan for ten minutes, stirring occasionally. Add the onion and 1 teaspoon salt and continue cooking until the meat mixture is dry and no longer pink (15 to 20 minutes). Add the *da'ah*, and pine nuts after the meat is fully cooked and combine. Set aside.

Step 4:

Preheat oven to 350 degrees.

Divide the eggplant slices evenly. Arrange half of them in a large baking pan. Put 2 to 3 tablespoons of the meat mixture on top of each slice. Press down slightly and top with another slice of eggplant.

If you are using quarters or baby eggplant instead of slices (see 'b' above), open the slit and stuff with meat mixture. Add the water to the tomato sauce or diced tomatoes; mix and pour over the eggplant.

Step 5:

Begin cooking Syrian rice (pages 187 or 189).

Step 6:

Bake eggplant uncovered for 30 minutes or until heated through.

BAKED LAMB STEW

Lahmeh Bil Furun *Yield: 6 to 8 servings*

The literal translation of *lahmeh bil furun* is "meat in the oven." It is similar to ratatouille, but includes chopped meat. Wiping your dish with pita makes a great finish. It is simple to prepare and very healthful. Feel free to experiment with compatible vegetables. It can be served over rice* with yogurt on the side.

*2½ pounds cubed (*shish kabob*) or ground (*kafta*) lamb*
1½ pounds green or yellow squash, diced
1 pound eggplant, diced
2 medium green bell peppers, cut into strips
3 large yellow onions, sliced
3 cups peeled and cubed red potatoes (optional)

Sauce
1 (28-ounce) can peeled whole tomatoes, crushed
1 (8-ounce) can tomato sauce
1 cup cold water
Kosher salt to taste
1 teaspoon allspice
1 teaspoon dried mint (optional)

Step 1:
Preheat the oven to 350 degrees.

Put the meat, squash, eggplant, peppers, onions, and potatoes (optional) in a large roasting pan.

Step 2:
Pour the tomatoes, tomato sauce, and water into a bowl. Mix in the salt, allspice and mint (optional).

Step 3:
Pour the sauce over the meat and vegetables in the roasting pan. Mix well and cover the pan tightly with foil. Bake in the oven 1 to 1½ hours or until the meat and vegetables are tender. Stir occasionally.

* Eliminate the side dish of rice if potatoes are used in the stew.

BAKED LAMB TARTARE

Kibbeh Sineyieh/Trabulsieh *Yield: 6 to 8 servings*

This is probably the most popular Syrian entrée and can be prepared two ways: either layered in a pan with stuffing between the layers (*kibbeh sineyieh*) or as stuffed egg-shaped meatballs (*kibbeh trabulsieh*), page 98. Both are popular and can be prepared beforehand and frozen for later use. The meatballs take slightly longer to prepare, and require some practice. They can also be served as an entrée or appetizer. If serving as an appetizer, make the meatballs smaller than the entrée size so that guests can dip them in yogurt.

Kibbeh is scrumptious served with a Syrian salad and/or a vegetable, yogurt and pita!

Kibbeh Sineyieh *(layered, with stuffing)*

½ cup rendered butter (page 186) plus ¼ cup diced
Kosher salt
*1½ pounds leanest cut of ground lamb (*hubra*)*
1½ cups #1 wheat
2 medium yellow onions (1 grated, 1 minced)
*1 pound ground lamb (*kafta*)*
½ cup pine nuts
1 teaspoon da'ah (page 19)

Step 1:
Put ½ cup butter in a 9 x 13 x 2-inch baking pan and place in a low temperature oven for 5 minutes or until melted. Remove the pan and swirl to cover the bottom and sides evenly. Let it cool and place in refrigerator until it hardens.

Step 2:
Add 1 teaspoon salt to the *hubra* and mix well. Refrigerate

Step 3:
Put the wheat in a bowl and cover with cold water. Drain through a fine strainer; rinse again; drain, return to bowl and refrigerate for ½ hour before using.

Step 4:

Put the grated onion into the bowl containing the wheat. Add the meat and knead well, wetting your hands in cold water occasionally while mixing until you have a somewhat firm, smooth texture, and pleasing flavor. Taste and add additional salt and/or water if needed. Refrigerate.

Step 5:

Sauté the *kafta* on low/medium heat for 10 minutes. Add the minced onion and continue cooking until the meat is no longer pink and mixture is dry. Mix occasionally. Add the nuts, ½ teaspoon salt, *da'ah*, and mix. Set aside to cool.

Step 6:

Preheat oven to 350 degrees

Divide the *kibbeh* in half. Take a small piece, flatten in the palm of your hand (hand should be slightly damp with cold water) and place in the pan. Spread out and smooth. Repeat the process until the bottom of the pan is completely covered with *kibbeh*. Cover with the stuffing; spread evenly and press down firmly. Use the remaining *kibbeh* for the top layer (use same procedure), and smooth. Cut into diamond-shape pieces and scatter the 4 tablespoons of butter on top. For cutting instructions, see recipe for baklava (page 197).

Bake for 30 to 40 minutes or until the top is golden brown.

Kibbeh Trabulsieh

Stuffed meatball *Yield: 35 medium-size meatballs*

Duplicate the ingredients from the *kibbeh sineyieh* recipe (page 96), and proceed with steps 1 through 5. Refrigerate the *kibbeh nayeh* before using.

Step 6:

Take a piece of *kibbeh nayeh* and roll into an egg-size ball. With your thumb, make a depression in the ball deep enough to accommodate 1 full tablespoon of stuffing, then seal. Sitto Helen always keeps a small bowl of ice water next to her so she can wet her hands while smoothing out the *kibbeh* balls. Make sure they are completely closed and smooth. You will have to roll them around in your hand quite a few times to do this. Ideally, the final shape should approximate an egg.

Step 7:

Place the *kibbeh balls* in the baking pan over the hardened butter and put a piece of butter on top of each meatball. You may need additional butter to finish topping each meatball.

Bake for 40 to 45 minutes or until lightly browned.

BAKED LAMB TARTARE STUFFED WITH WHOLE EGG

Kibbeh Ba'id *Yield: 8 servings*

Accompanied by a salad, this *kibbeh* entrée makes a great luncheon dish. Seasoning the eggs with salt and allspice add a special touch. Serve cold or warm in pita with lettuce or cut into quarters and eat with your fingers. Great for picnics!

4 extra-large eggs, hard boiled
Kosher salt
Allspice
1 pound leanest cut of ground lamb (hubra)
¾ cup #1 wheat
1 medium yellow onion, grated

Step 1:
Shell the eggs and sprinkle all over with ¼ teaspoon salt and allspice. Set aside.

Step 2:
Add ½ teaspoon salt to the *hubra*, and mix well. Refrigerate.

Step 3:
Put the wheat in a bowl and cover with cold water. Drain through a fine strainer; rinse again; drain, return to bowl and refrigerate for ½ hour before using.

Step 4:
Put the grated onion in the bowl containing the wheat. Add the meat and knead well, wetting your hands occasionally while mixing until you have a somewhat firm, smooth texture, and pleasing flavor. Taste and add additional salt and/or water if needed.

Continued

Step 5:

Divide the *kibbeh nayeh* into 4 parts. Spread one into an oval shape large enough to encompass an egg. Place the egg on top and close the *kibbeh* around it. Wet your hands slightly to smooth evenly and make sure there are no openings. Repeat until all the *kibbeh* is used.

Step 6:

Bring a pot of water to a boil; place the stuffed *kibbeh* in the water; cover with lid tilted and simmer 5 minutes or until the meat is no longer pink. Pour gently into a colander. Set aside to cool, then slice or cut into quarters and serve.

BAKED MACARONI AND LAMB

Macaron'eh ou Lahmeh *Yield: 6 servings*

When we were kids our mothers prepared a pasta dish we called "Syrian macaroni." Not until we dined in Italian restaurants as adults did we realize that macaroni was really Italian.

Our sauce, however, is somewhat different. We add onions and bell pepper; use lamb instead of beef, and allspice instead of black pepper. We also sprinkle cinnamon over the pasta and occasionally add bits of butter on top before baking.

2 tablespoons olive or canola oil
2 large yellow onions, minced
1 medium green or red bell pepper, minced
2 cloves garlic, minced
*1 pound coarsely chopped lamb (*mafroomah*)*
1 (28-ounce) can peeled whole tomatoes, crushed
1 (6-ounce) can tomato paste
1 (8-ounce) can tomato sauce
½ cup cold water
Kosher salt to taste
1 teaspoon allspice
1 pound rotini pasta, or any similar pasta
4 tablespoons (½ stick) salted butter, cut into bits (optional)
1 teaspoon cinnamon

Step 1:

Heat oil in a saucepan. Add the onions and pepper and sauté until softened. Add the garlic and sauté another minute. Add the meat; mix and cook 10 to 15 minutes or until the meat is no longer pink and the mixture is dry. Mix in the tomatoes, tomato paste, tomato sauce, water, salt, and allspice. Bring to a boil, lower the heat and simmer for 1 hour.

Continued

Step 2:

Preheat oven to 350 degrees.

Step 3:

Boil the pasta for 7 minutes **only**. Drain in a colander and spread evenly in a large baking pan. Pour the sauce over the pasta and mix. Scatter the butter bits (optional) over the top of the pasta and sprinkle cinnamon over it. Cover tightly with foil and bake for approximately 30 minutes **or** uncover after 20 minutes and put under the broiler for 10 minutes or until the top is crisp. Either way is tasty. Mix once or twice while baking. If it seems dry, add an additional ¼ cup of water, and mix.

BRAISED BONELESS LEG OF LAMB IN TOMATO SAUCE WITH PEAS

Fag'dah *Yield: 8 servings*

Leg of lamb Syrian-style is a formal meal often reserved for feasts such as Easter or Christmas when it is ceremoniously sliced at the table by the head of the family. It can be prepared two ways: cooked in tomato sauce with peas (*fag'dah*) or cooked in vinegar (*dor'bough*). Both versions are quite easy to prepare and make an impressive display when served on a bed of Syrian rice or wheat (*burghol*), and garnished with parsley. They can also be served with rice or wheat on the side.

A Middle Eastern butcher will often spice the lamb before rolling and tying it. If this is the case, we recommend using half the amount of spices indicated in the ingredients. Also, supermarkets often carry a boned leg of lamb in a net casing. This is fine to use since the casing holds the meat together. Slits can be made right through the casing but be careful not to tear it.

The tomato sauce and vinegar versions of this dish taste quite different, but are equally popular.

1 (5-pound) lean leg of lamb, boned and tied.
5 cloves garlic, crushed
2 tablespoons da'ah (page 19)
Kosher salt
2 tablespoons olive oil
1 (28-ounce) can peeled whole tomatoes, crushed
*2 cups drained green peas**

Garnish
2 tablespoons flat-leaf parsley

Step 1:
Remove any excess fat and put numerous slits in the lamb. Mix the garlic and *da'ah*, and put into the slits. Salt the lamb lightly.

*If frozen peas are used, simply thaw, drain, and add to the sauce.

Step 2:

Heat the oil or butter in a heavy pot. Add the lamb and brown well on all sides, approximately 35 minutes. Remove the lamb and drain excess fat. Leave the scrapings in the pot and return the lamb.

Step 3:

Add the tomatoes, cover and simmer 2 hours** or until the meat is pink inside. When the lamb is cooked, remove from the pot, place on a platter and cover tightly with foil until ready to slice. Reserve the juices.

**If you would like to remove excess fat from the sauce, remove the lamb after 1 hour of simmering and refrigerate the meat and sauce separately. The fat in the sauce will jell and can be removed easily with a slotted spoon. Return the lamb to the pot with the sauce; bring to a slow boil and continue cooking.

Step 4:

Begin cooking Syrian rice (page 187 or 189).

Step 5:

Add the peas to the reserved meat juices and heat through. Serve the sauce separately in a bowl or on top of the lamb after it is sliced.

Vinegared Boneless Leg of Lamb with Cracked Wheat

Dor'bough *Yield: 8 servings*

Duplicate the ingredients for *fag'dah*, (page 103), but substitute 2 cups of vinegar plus 1½ cups cold water for the tomatoes.

Follow steps 1 through 4 for *fag'dah*. When cooked, pour out all but 1 cup of the juices into a measuring cup; cover the pot and set aside.* Immediately prepare the *burghol* using the reserved liquids. *Dor'bough* is usually served with *burghol* rather than rice and topped with chickpeas.

*The lamb should stay warm in the pot until the full meal is ready to be served. Ten minutes before the *burghol* is cooked, check the meat. If you feel it is not warm enough turn on the heat and simmer until heated through.

For *burghol* preparation see recipe page 181, substituting water/vinegar mixture for broth. For 1 cup wheat, use mixture and, if necessary, additional water to equal 2¼ cups. For 8 servings, use 4½ cups liquid in a 2:1 ratio of water to vinegar and double other ingredients. Top the *burghol* with one 15-ounce can of chickpeas, heated and drained. Garnish with chopped parsley and/or grape tomatoes.

BROILED LAMB TARTARE WITH MINT

Kibbeh Asieck *Yield: 4 to 5 servings*

These finger-shape, aromatic delicacies can be freshly prepared or made with leftover *kibbeh nayeh* from any *kibbeh* recipe. They are quick and easy to make and can be served in a variety of ways. They are delicious in pita topped with yogurt, *baba ghanouj*, *hummus* or freshly chopped tomatoes. As a main dish, they can be served with a Syrian salad, yogurt and pita or cut into pieces and heated in a soup of your choice (chicken noodle, tomato, chicken and rice, for example).

4 tablespoons rendered butter (page 186)
½ teaspoon kosher salt
1 pound leanest cut of ground lamb (hubra)
¾ cup #1 wheat
1 medium yellow onion, grated
3 tablespoons dried mint
1 teaspoon allspice (optional)

Utensil
1 skewer, optional

Step 1:
Put the rendered butter in a 9 x 13 x 2-inch baking pan and place in a 350 degree oven for 5 minutes or until melted. Remove the pan and swirl it to cover the bottom evenly. Cool, and place in refrigerator until the butter hardens.

Step 2:
Add the salt to the *hubra* and mix well. Refrigerate.

Step 3:
Put the wheat in a bowl and cover with cold water. Drain through a fine strainer; rinse again; drain, return to bowl and refrigerate for ½ hour before using.

Step 4:

Put the grated onion in the bowl containing the wheat. Add the meat, mint and allspice (optional) and knead well, wetting your hands in cold water occasionally while mixing until you have a somewhat firm, smooth texture, and pleasing flavor. Taste and add additional salt and/or water if needed.

Step 5:

Take a piece of meat the size of a small egg, wrap around the skewer or roll in your hands smoothing it into the shape of a small cigar (4-inches long, 1 inch in diameter). If you use a skewer, slide the meat off and place in the pan. Broil for 3 to 5 minutes on each side or until lightly browned.

BUTTER-STUFFED LAMB MEATBALLS AND QUINCE STEW

Kibbeh Sifejileah | *Yield: 8 servings*

The quince is a tree with white flowers and an aromatic, apple-like fruit that is native to western Asia. The fruit is edible only when cooked. Preparation time is lengthy, but well worth the effort.

*2 pounds cubed (*shish kabob*) lamb*
Kosher salt
*1 pound leanest cut of ground lamb (*hubra*)*
¾ cup #1 wheat
1 medium yellow onion, grated
¾ cup (1½ sticks) salted butter, cold
Allspice
Cinnamon
6 quinces, peeled and each cut into 4 pieces
1 cup sugar
½ teaspoon red food coloring, mixed with a few drops of cold water
2 tablespoons fresh lemon juice

Step 1:

Put the cubed lamb in a pot and cover with cold water, about 1 inch over the meat. Cover and bring to a slow boil. Immediately pour into a colander to remove the greasy residue. Rinse the meat and return to the pot. Cover again with fresh water and bring to a slow boil. Lower the heat, cover with lid tilted, and simmer until the meat is tender, 40 to 45 minutes. When the meat is cooked, drain in a colander, and refrigerate in a bowl.

Step 2:

Add ½ teaspoon salt to the meat and mix well. Refrigerate. Put the wheat in a bowl and cover with cold water. Drain through a fine strainer; rinse again; drain, return to bowl and refrigerate for ½ hour.

Step 3:

Put the grated onion into the bowl containing the wheat. Add the meat and knead well, wetting your hands in cold water occasionally while mixing until you have a somewhat firm, smooth texture, and pleasing flavor. Taste and add additional salt and/or water if needed. Refrigerate.

Step 4:

Cut the butter into bits. Place on a large dish/platter in a single layer. Sprinkle the pieces generously with allspice and cinnamon until they are completely covered. Take a piece of *kibbeh nayeh* and roll into a walnut-size ball. Using your thumb, make a depression large enough to accommodate a piece of seasoned butter. Put a piece of butter into the opening and close the top. Keep a bowl of ice water next to you. Wet your hands occasionally and roll the meat in your hands until completely closed and smooth.

Step 5:

Bring a pot of lightly salted cold water to a boil. Put the *kibbeh* balls in the water and when they rise to the top lower the heat. Simmer 3 minutes. Drain in a colander, and refrigerate in a bowl.

Step 6:

Put the fruit and sugar in a medium-size pot; cover with cold water, and mix. Bring to a slow boil. Add the food coloring, mix again, and lower the heat. Cover with lid tilted and simmer for 30 to 45 minutes until tender, piercing with a fork to test. The fruit should be soft, not mushy. When cooked, turn off the heat.

Step 7:

Put the cooked lamb cubes, *kibbeh* balls, and lemon juice in the pot with the fruit. Add the salt and mix. Simmer until the meat is heated through. Pour into individual bowls and serve with pita.

CHICKEN, LAMB, AND VEGETABLE COMBO

Mloukhiyeh *Yield: 10 to 12 servings*

Our cousin Barbara Sayour, whose father hailed from Damascus, where this meal is popular, offered this recipe to us. Her mother, our Aunt Jeanette always invited her brothers, Richard and Charlie, for dinner whenever she prepared this feast. They just loved it! Preparation time is extensive but if you want to try something different, this meal is well worth it.

Mloukhiyeh, imported from Egypt, is the primary vegetable in this recipe. It has an unfamiliar glutinous (sticky) quality. Most Middle Eastern stores sell it either dried or frozen. We recommend frozen since it takes less time to cook. The *kibbeh*, chicken, and lamb shanks can be prepared the day before serving or prepared and frozen for later use. If frozen, thaw; reheat and serve. Cooking the meat beforehand cuts preparation time the day the meal is served.

Because of the effort involved, it is more efficient to make a large quantity. Leftovers can always be reheated and served again. In some Middle Eastern countries, *mloukhiyeh* is prepared without any lamb, just chicken. This is a personal choice.

Rice

6 cups cold water
3 cups uncooked white rice
1 teaspoon kosher salt

Kibbeh Nayeh

½ cup rendered butter (page 186)
1 teaspoon kosher salt
*2 pounds leanest cut of ground lamb (*hubra*)*
1½ cups #1 wheat
1 large yellow onion, grated

Stuffing

*1 pound ground lamb (*kafta*)*
1 medium onion, minced
½ cup pine nuts
1 teaspoon kosher salt
1 teaspoon da'ah (page 19)
4 tablespoons rendered butter (page 186), diced

Lamb Shanks

6 lamb shanks (1½ pounds each)
6 cloves garlic, slivered
Kosher salt
3 teaspoons allspice
3 tablespoons olive oil

Chicken

2 (4-pound) chickens
4 cloves garlic, crushed
5 (14-ounce) packages frozen mloukhiyeh
4 medium yellow onions, minced
6 cups wine vinegar

4 large or 8 small pita, toasted until golden brown and broken into bite-size pieces (before toasting, separate the tops from the bottoms)

Step 1:

Pour the water into a wide, deep pot and bring to a boil. Add the rice, 1-teaspoon salt, and mix. Lower the heat and cover the pot. Simmer 20 minutes or until the rice is tender. When the rice is cooked, turn off the heat and set aside.

Step 2:

Put ½-cup butter into a 9 x 13 x 2-inch baking pan and place in a low temperature oven for a few minutes or until melted. Remove the pan; cool and place into the refrigerator until the butter hardens.

Continued

Step 3:

Add 1-teaspoon salt to the *hubra*, and mix well. Refrigerate. Place the wheat into a bowl and cover with cold water. Drain into a fine strainer; rinse again; drain and refrigerate for at least ½ hour.

Put the grated onion into the bowl containing the wheat. Add the meat and knead well, wetting your hands in cold water occasionally while mixing until you have a somewhat firm, smooth texture, and pleasing flavor. Taste and add additional salt and/or water if needed. Refrigerate.

Step 4:

Sauté the *kafta* on low/medium heat for 10 minutes. Add the minced onion and continue cooking until the meat is no longer pink and mixture is dry. This should take approximately 15 minutes. Add the nuts, salt, *da'ah*, and mix.

Step 5:

Preheat oven to 350 degrees.

Step 6:

Divide the *kibbeh* meat in half. Wet your hands slightly with cold water; take a small piece of meat and flatten in the palm of your hand. Place into the buttered pan, spread out, and smooth. Repeat the process until the bottom of the pan is completely covered with the meat. Put the *kafta* stuffing over the *kibbeh*; spread out and press down firmly. Place the remaining *kibbeh* on top (repeat procedure) and smooth. Cut into diamond-shape pieces and scatter the 4 tablespoons butter on top. For cutting instructions, see recipe for baklava (page 197).

Bake for 30 to 40 minutes or until the top is golden brown.

Step 7:

Put slits into the lamb and insert the slivered garlic. Salt the meat lightly and rub ½ teaspoon of allspice over each individual shank. Heat the oil in a wide, deep pot. Add the meat and brown on all sides. Add 2 cups of cold water; cover and simmer 1½ hours or until tender. Remove the meat from the bones and shred. Refrigerate for later use.

tep 8:

Wash the chickens thoroughly. Place into a large pot and cover with cold water. Bring to a boil; lower the heat and remove the residue on top. Simmer 1 hour or until thoroughly cooked. Remove the chickens from the pot and set aside. Pour the broth through a fine strainer into a bowl and set aside for later use. The broth should yield approximately 3 quarts. While the chickens are still warm, remove the meat from the bones and shred. Refrigerate for later use.

tep 9:

Place the chicken broth into a pot and add the crushed garlic. Remove the *mloukhiyeh* from the frozen package (do not thaw) and place into the broth. Bring to a slow boil and simmer 10 minutes, no longer. If it is cooked too long, the vegetable will sink to the bottom; you want it to float in the broth. Turn off the heat and set aside.

tep 10:

Add the minced onions to the vinegar and set aside.

tep 11:

To serve, place a few pieces of pita on the bottom of each soup bowl and top with a few pieces of *kibbeh*, a small amount of rice and a few pieces of lamb meat. Top with ½ cup of *mloukhiyeh*/broth, and a few pieces of chicken. Cover with rice and *mloukhiyeh*/broth again. Top with ½ cup of the onion and vinegar mixture.

CHICKEN AND OLIVE COMBO

Jaj Zatoon ou Riz *Yield: 6 to 8 servings*

This favored entrée is a unique mixture of chicken and olives. Served wit Syrian rice, it presents itself beautifully at the dinner table garnished wit pine nuts.

For perfect timing, steps 3, 4 and 5 should be done simultaneously. The brot from the cooked chicken will be used throughout the recipe, so do not discar any of it.

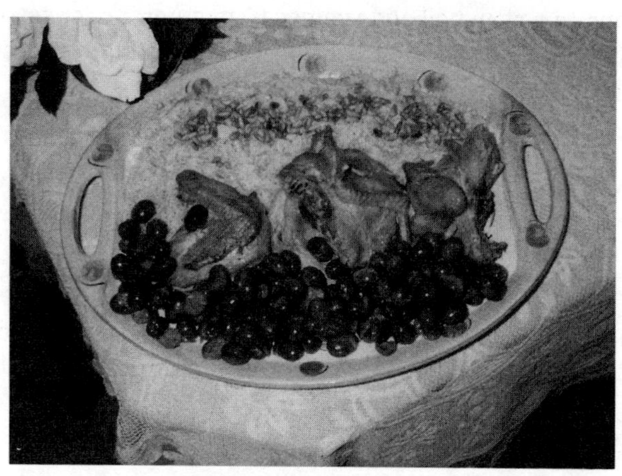

2 pounds small "Naphilion" olives (broken/cracked green Greek olives)
5-pounds chicken, whole or quartered
1 yellow onion, diced
1 (8-ounce) can tomato sauce

Step 1:

Remove the pits from the olives; rinse well and soak in cold water overnight to remove the salty, bitter taste.

Step 2:

Wash the chicken and put in a large pot. Cover with cold water. Bring to a boil and lower the heat. Skim the residue from the top of the water while cooking and discard. Add the onion and cover with lid tilted.

Simmer for approximately 1 hour or until thoroughly cooked. Remove the chicken from the broth and set aside. Pour the broth into a bowl through a fine strainer and set aside for later use. If you wish to remove the hardened layer of fat from the broth before using, prepare the chicken beforehand and refrigerate the broth overnight.

tep 3:

Preheat oven to 400 degrees.

tep 4:

Place the whole chicken or pieces, skin side up, in a baking pan. Pour 1 cup of reserved broth over the chicken. Bake for 25 minutes; baste occasionally, then put the pan into the broiler for a few minutes until the skin is lightly crisp. Be careful not to overcook.

tep 5:

Begin cooking Syrian rice (page 187 or 189).

tep 6:

Drain the water from the olives; rinse, and put them into a saucepan with ½ cup broth. Sauté 10 minutes then add an additional 1½ cups of broth, and the tomato sauce. Mix; cover with lid tilted; bring to slow boil; lower the heat, and simmer an additional 15 minutes.

tep 7:

When serving, place the chicken and rice on separate platters and the olives in a bowl. For a more elegant effect, you can place the chicken in the middle of a large platter with rice along one side and olives on the other. Garnish with pine nuts and parsley. Serve with pita and enjoy!

For leftovers, remove the chicken from the bones, and mix with the olives and sauce. Heat and serve over Syrian rice.

CHICKEN, WHEAT AND VEGETABLE COMBO

Jaj Burghol ou Kuthra *Yield: 4 servings as a main course, 6 as a side dish*

This was originally a vegetarian dish. Virginia thought it might be tastier with chicken so she added some and it worked very well. It is terrific either way.

Serve, garnished with lightly toasted pine nuts, a Syrian salad, and pita.

4 tablespoons canola or olive oil
1 medium yellow onion, minced
4 cloves garlic, minced
1½ cups #4 wheat
3 cups chicken broth
1 teaspoon kosher salt
½ teaspoon black pepper
½ pound fresh white button mushrooms, sliced
3 medium carrots, diced
2 cups green peas (if frozen, cook per package directions and drain well; if canned, drain well.)
1 cup diced cooked chicken, preferably white meat (optional)
¼ cup chopped flat-leaf parsley

Step 1:

Pour 2 tablespoons of oil into a heavy saucepan and heat. Add the onion and sauté for 5 minutes or until softened. Add the garlic and sauté 2 minutes. Add the wheat and sauté 2 minutes. Add the broth, salt and pepper and bring to a boil. Reduce heat, cover, and simmer 30 to 35 minutes or until the liquid is absorbed and the wheat is tender.

tep 2:

In another pan heat the remaining 2 tablespoons of oil. Add the mushrooms and carrots and sauté 10 minutes or until tender. Add the peas and chicken (optional) and heat through.

tep 3:

Gently stir the vegetable/chicken combination into the cooked wheat mixture. Stir in the parsley. Taste and adjust seasonings if desired. Transfer to a serving dish.

COLD FISH WITH TAHINI

Sem'ek Taratoor *Yield: 6 to 8 servings*

This seafood recipe is one of our cousin Marilyn Jerro Tadross' specialtie Marilyn serves *sem'ek taratoor* at many family get-togethers, always to th great satisfaction of her guests.

It can be served at a luncheon or buffet, as an appetizer or entrée. The enti preparation can be completed the day before serving.

Present with a Syrian salad or potato salad, vegetable, and pita as an entré As an appetizer, serve on pita, melba toast, or a cracker of your choice.

1 (4-pound) red snapper or sea bass, whole or fillets

Poaching marinade
1/4 cup fresh lemon juice
1/2 cup white wine
1/2 teaspoon kosher salt
1/4 cup olive oil

Dressing
4 cloves garlic
1 teaspoon kosher salt
2 cups tahini
1 cup cold water
1/2 cup fresh lemon juice

Garnish
1 black olive
1 medium cucumber, thinly sliced
1/2 cup pomegranate seeds
1/4 cup pine nuts, toasted
1 large yellow onion, thinly sliced and sautéed in 1 tablespoon of oil until crispy
1/4 cup chopped flat-leaf parsley
1 lemon, thinly sliced

Step 1:

Buy the fish cleaned and scaled. Leave the head on but remove the eyes. Slash skin on the body of the fish on both sides. If using fillets less cooking time is required. Do not slash.

Step 2:

Preheat oven to 350 degrees.

Step 3:

Pour the lemon juice and wine into a bowl; add the salt; mix and set aside. Coat a baking pan with the oil; place the fish in the pan and cover with the marinade. Bake uncovered for 30 minutes or until the fish is cooked at the thickest part. If using fillets, be careful not to overcook. They poach faster than whole fish. If using a whole fish, remove the head, skin and bones while it is still warm and flake the flesh. Refrigerate the head if you wish to use it later when reforming the fish. Put the flaked fish in a bowl, cover and refrigerate.

Step 4:

Mash the garlic and salt together and set aside. Combine the tahini and water in a bowl. Add the lemon juice and garlic/salt mixture and mix well with a wooden spoon. The marinade should have a creamy consistency and taste slightly tart. To thicken add small amounts of water; to thin add small amounts of lemon juice.

Step 5:

Remove the fish from the refrigerator and, on a platter, form into the shape of a fish. Place the head where it normally would be, an olive where the eye would be. Use cucumber slices to simulate scales. Spread ½ of the dressing over the fish and follow with the pomegranate seeds and nuts. Decorate the edges of the fish with the onion, parsley and lemon slices. Serve the remainder of the dressing on the side. To serve the next day, just cover and refrigerate. Bring to room temperature before serving.

CUBED LAMB AND OKRA STEW

Riz ou Bameh *Yield: 4 to 5 servings*

Though not the most popular vegetable in the United States, okra is delicio prepared this way. For tenderness, fresh okra should be small. Baby froz okra is always a safe bet. As with *riz ou fowleh*, this meal should be served wi Syrian rice. You can arrange the rice along the circumference of a colorful plat and mound the okra in the center. Serve with pita and yogurt on the side. V recommend preparing the meat mixture and rice at the same time.

1 tablespoon olive oil
1 large yellow onion, minced
2 cloves garlic, minced
*1 pound cubed or coarsely chopped (*mafroomah*) lam*
1 tablespoon coriander
1 teaspoon kosher salt
1 teaspoon allspice
1 teaspoon sugar
1/4 cup fresh or bottled lemon juice
1 teaspoon pomegranate molasses (page 185) (optiona
1 pound fresh okra, stems removed or 2 (10-ounce) packages frozen okra, thawed
1 (14.5-ounce) can stewed tomatoes
1 cup cold water

Step 1:
Heat the oil in a large skillet. Add the onion, and garlic and sauté 5 minutes or until softened.

Step 2:
Add the meat, coriander, salt, allspice, sugar, lemon juice, molasses (optional) and cook on low heat for 10 minutes. Stir occasionally.

Step 3:
Begin cooking Syrian rice (page 187 or 189).

Step 4:
Add the okra, tomatoes and water. Cover with lid tilted and cook until the meat and vegetables are tender (approximately 20 minutes).

EGG AND LAMB BRAIN PATTIES

Ir'jeh Zwaz *Yield: approximately 20 patties*

Eaten at room temperature, this luncheon entrée can be prepared a day or two before serving. It can also be reheated lightly in a microwave. Serve in pita and top with tomato slices and lettuce and again, do not forget Sitto Helen's garlic pickles (page 59).

6 or 7 lamb brains
10 jumbo eggs
1 tablespoon allspice
1 teaspoon salt
Canola oil for frying

Utensil

Heavy-duty pan with cavities similar to a poached egg pan. Called ir'jeh *pans, they can be purchased at most Middle Eastern markets. Try to find pans with deep cavities.*

Step 1:

Rinse the brains well and remove as much of the membranes as possible. Place in boiling water; lower the heat and simmer approximately 10 minutes. Drain and cool. Cut into small cubes and set aside.

Step 2:

Crack the eggs into a bowl and whip. Add the brains, allspice, salt, and mix. The consistency should be thick.

Step 3:

Pour approximately 1 tablespoon of oil into each cup of the pan and heat. Add additional oil as needed while frying. Add 2 tablespoons egg mixture or enough to fill the cup. Fry until nicely browned, approximately 3 minutes on each side. Remove and drain well on paper towels.

Ir'jeh zwaz can also be baked in the oven. Use a 9 x 2-inch square pan; coat the bottom with 5 tablespoons canola oil then pour the egg mixture in. Bake in a preheated 350 degree oven for 30 minutes or until lightly browned on top. Let cool and cut into 2 x 2-inch squares before serving.

EGGPLANT STUFFED WITH LAMB AND RICE IN TOMATO LEMON SAUCE

Bantenjan Mahshee *Yield: 8 to 10 servings*

Another highly flavored eggplant dish that can be eaten alone or with yogurt, fresh vegetables, and pita. It tastes delicious if you slit the eggplant and place a few dabs of yogurt on top. Best to stuff the eggplant the day you cook it. If you like eggplant, this dish will be one of your favorites.

If you have lamb bones place them in the pot under the eggplant before cooking. They add flavor and are a tasty treat themselves.

Instead of discarding the eggplant innards, Philip suggests using them to make *baba ghanouj*. Place them in a shallow bowl, add a small amount of water, cover and cook in a microwave until tender. The innards may appear darker than usual, but they taste just fine. Then follow the *baba ghanouj* recipe (page 53). You can also cook the innards in tomato sauce and serve as a vegetable dish.

5 pounds eggplant (approximately 15 miniature ones)
7 or 8 lamb bones (optional)
2 pounds coarsely chopped lamb (mafroomah)
1¼ cups uncooked white rice
1 (8-ounce) can tomato sauce
¼ cup cold water
1 teaspoon kosher salt
2 teaspoons allspice

Sauce
1 (28-ounce) can peeled whole tomatoes, crushed
2 cups bottled lemon juice
¼ cup dried mint
1 head or 10 cloves garlic, crushed
2 tablespoons pomegranate molasses (page 185)
1 teaspoon kosher salt

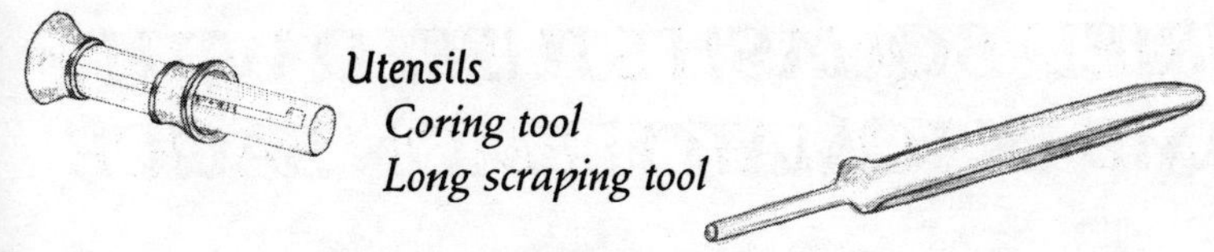

Step 1:

Scrub, rinse and dry the eggplants. Remove and discard the stems and cut 1 inch off the tops.

Step 2:

Using the tools, gradually and carefully core and scrape out the eggplant innards. Remove as much of the inside as you can, but leave the skin thick enough to retain its shape without collapsing. Be careful not to penetrate the sides or the bottom. Torn sides can be sealed with string. Just wrap around the wound and knot.

Step 3:

Mix the meat, rice, tomato sauce, water, salt, allspice and stuff into each eggplant.

Step 4:

Mix the tomatoes, lemon juice, mint, garlic, molasses, and salt and set aside.

Step 5:

Place the eggplants in a wide, deep pot, preferably over lamb bones. Pour the sauce over them and place an inverted dish on top to prevent shifting. Cover and bring the liquid to a full boil. Lower the heat and simmer 45 minutes. Before turning off the heat, remove some of the stuffing with a fork and taste to see if the rice is tender. Also, push fork tines into the vegetable to check for tenderness. If not, continue cooking another 5 to 10 minutes. When completely cooked, close the heat, tilt the cover, and pour the juices into a bowl. Use the juices to reheat leftovers. Recover the pot and let stand 15 minutes. Carefully remove the eggplants; place on a platter and serve.

FRIED SQUASH STUFFED WITH LAMB IN TOMATO LEMON SAUCE

Shuk al Nahshee *Yield: 6 servings*

This is a mouth-watering variation on the Syrian culinary tradition of stuffing vegetables with lamb. Serve with Syrian rice and garnish with toasted pine nuts.

Steps 1, 2 and 3 can be completed the day before serving.

5 pounds thin and small zucchini squash
Vegetable shortening for frying
*2 pounds ground lamb (*kafta*)*
½ cup pine nuts
½ cup flat-leaf parsley, minced
1 teaspoon kosher salt
1 teaspoon da'ah (page 19)

Sauce
1 (28-ounce) can peeled whole tomatoes, crushed
1 (8-ounce) can tomato sauce
¼ cup lemon juice (fresh or bottled)
1 teaspoon kosher salt
1 teaspoon sugar

Utensils
Coring tool
Long scraping tool

Step 1:
Cut off the stems plus ¼ inch of the squash and discard. Rinse the squash and pat dry. Insert the coring tool, and remove the innards. Use the scraper on the inner sides to clean out the remainder, but do not scoop out as much as you would for *coussa mahshee*. Since you are frying the squash, the outside flesh should be about ⅛-inch thick so the vegetable does not break while frying.

If you wish, save some of the innards, fry and cook in the sauce with the squash.

Step 2:

Mix the meat, nuts, parsley, salt, and *da'ah* and fill the squash to about ½ inch from the mouth. Gently insert the mixture with your thumb. If there is leftover mixture shape into small meatballs; fry until golden brown, drain well on paper towels and add to the sauce with the squash.

Step 3:

In a large frying pan melt enough shortening to at least a ½ inch depth. Add additional shortening as needed. Fry each squash 15 minutes on each side on medium heat or until browned. Use a spatula to remove the squash or they may break. Place a few sheets of paper towel on a large dish or platter and place the squash on top to drain.

Step 4:

Begin cooking Syrian rice (page 187 or 189).

Step 5:

Pour the tomatoes, tomato sauce, lemon juice, salt, and sugar into a large pot. Cover with lid tilted and simmer for 15 minutes. Individually place the squash carefully in the sauce and simmer for ½ hour or until the squash is heated through.

GRAPE LEAVES FILLED WITH LAMB AND RICE

Yebrat *Yield: 60 yebrat or 8 servings*

This well-known dish is sold in many American supermarkets and savored at sophisticated parties. Syrian grape leaves include lamb, spices and tomato sauce. *Yebrat* is sometimes used as an appetizer, though it is traditionally served as a main meal with *kibbeh nayeh*, especially during the holidays. Delicious hot, they can also be served at room temperature as a finger food. Simply garnish with garlic and lemon wedges.

Yebrat can be prepared and frozen uncooked for later use. Stack tightly together in a plastic container and freeze. Leftovers can also be frozen in their juices.

*2 pounds coarse chopped lamb (*mafroomah*)*
1¼ cups uncooked white rice
1 (8-ounce) can tomato sauce
1 teaspoon kosher salt
2 teaspoons allspice
1¼ cup cold water
½ pound grape leaves or more as needed (see Basic Guidelines, page 29, for leaf preparation)
8 lamb bones (optional)
2 cups bottled lemon juice or a combination of 2 cups lemon juice and 1 cup tomato sauce

Step 1:

Mix the meat, rice, tomato sauce, salt, allspice, and ¼ cup of water and set aside.

Step 2:

Place a grape leaf vein side up on a flat surface and put 1 to 2 tablespoons of stuffing across the widest part, but not to the edge of the leaf. Do not overstuff; it may cause the leaf to rip while rolling or when the rice expands when cooking. Fold the sides over the ends of the stuffing and roll gently from the bottom of the leaf until sealed.

Step 3:

If you are going to use bones, place them in a deep, wide pot. Put the stuffed leaves on top of the bones, seam side down, tightly together. Place the garlic pieces between the layers.

Step 4:

Mix 1 cup water and lemon juice and pour over the stuffed leaves. Place an inverted dish on top to prevent shifting. Cover, and bring the mixture to a boil. Lower the heat and simmer 35 minutes or until the rice is tender. Taste a grape leaf to see if the rice is cooked. As soon as the grape leaves are cooked, turn off the heat, tilt the cover, and pour the juices into a bowl. Use the juices to reheat leftovers. Recover the pot and let stand 15 minutes. Carefully remove the grape leaves, one at a time. Serve stacked on a platter.

A fancier serving alternative would be to prepare the grape leaves with bones as in step 2, filling the pot to the brim. After cooking, pour out the juice, hold an inverted round dinner plate or platter over the pot and turn upside down very carefully. The bones and leaves should come out stacked neatly.

Garnish with cooked garlic cloves and serve with fresh vegetables, *kibbeh nayeh* (page 56), pita and/or yogurt.

How to roll grape leaves

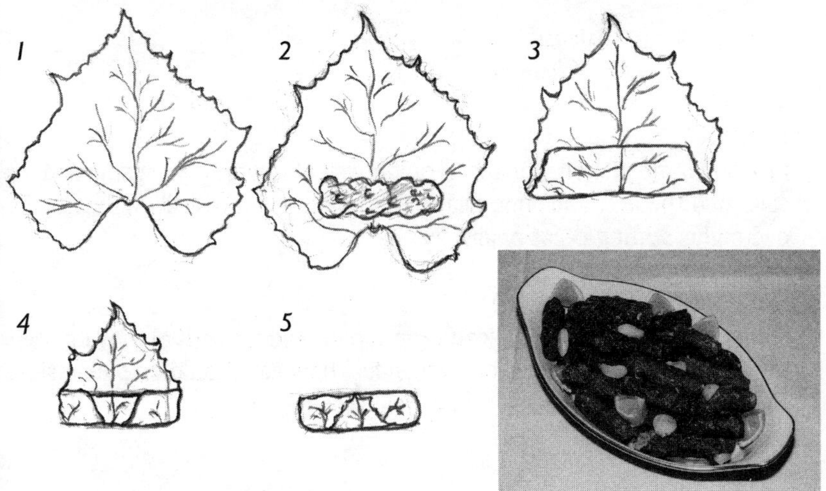

GRILLED LAMB LIVER

Mer'lat *Yield: 4 to 6 servings*

Lamb liver was a staple when we were growing up, but now it is difficult to find a butcher who carries it. As a grilled dish, its preparation is similar to *shish kabob*, but without the vegetables. For flavor, we used to alternate the liver with pieces of lamb fat and onions, but with today's lite diets, we no longer use the fat.

Mer'lat goes very well with *kibbeh nayeh* (page 56), a Syrian salad, Syrian rice (page 187 or 189) and pita.

1/4 cup olive oil
1/2 teaspoon coriander
1 small yellow onion, grated
1/4 cup chopped celery leaves
2 tablespoons dried mint
2 cloves garlic, minced
1 teaspoon kosher salt
1 whole piece lamb liver, rinsed and cubed
2 lamb hearts, rinsed and cubed (optional)
3 pieces lamb fat, cubed
6 tiny white onions

Utensil
Skewers

Step 1:
In a bowl, mix the oil, coriander, onion, celery leaves, mint, garlic and salt. Add the liver and lamb hearts (optional) and mix well. Marinate overnight, stirring occasionally.

Step 2:
Alternate the meat cubes, hearts (optional), and fat with onions on skewers and grill a few minutes on each side. The meat should be pink inside. This tastes much better rare than well done.

GROUND LAMB AND CRACKED WHEAT COMBO

Burghol bil Lahmeh *Yield: 4 to 5 servings*

This is an inexpensive, healthful and tasty meal. Philip's Dad, Mitchell, loved it to the point where he trusted no one but himself to make it. Served with plain yogurt to cool the palate, it begs to be swiped up with pita. It is also delicious served with a yogurt salad.

For an attractive presentation, place grape tomatoes along the rim of the platter.

*1 pound coarsely chopped lamb (*mafroomah*)*
1 cup diced yellow onions
1 teaspoon allspice
1 teaspoon kosher salt
1½ cups cold water or 1½ cups chicken broth
2 cups #4 wheat, rinsed and drained
3 cups peeled whole tomatoes, crushed or stewed or diced fresh tomatoes
2 tablespoons salted butter
1 (8-ounce) can chickpeas, drained (optional)

Step 1:

Put the meat and onions in a deep, wide pot and sauté a few minutes or until the onions are softened. Add the allspice and salt; mix and continue cooking until the meat is no longer pink and the mixture is fairly dry.

Step 2:

Add the water or broth, wheat, and tomatoes to the pot. Stir; cover and bring to a boil. Lower the flame and simmer 45 minutes or until the wheat is tender. Taste the wheat to see if it is still hard. If so, take a fork and push through the wheat to the bottom of the pot. If the bottom is dry, add ¼ cup of additional water/broth or more as needed and continue cooking until the wheat is tender.

Add the butter and chickpeas (optional). Mix well before serving.

GROUND LAMB AND GREEN BEAN STEW

Riz ou Fowleh *Yield: 6 servings*

This stew-like meal is inexpensive, easy to prepare and especially attractiv when served on colorful plates with Syrian rice. Philip arranges the rice alon the circumference of a decorative platter and mounds the meat and bean (*fowleh* mixture in the center. Garnish rice with pine nuts. Serve with yogurt.

We recommend preparing the meat mixture and the rice at the same time.

1 tablespoon olive oil
1 large yellow onion, diced
2 cloves garlic, minced
*1 pound ground (*kafta*) or cubed (*shish kabob*) lam*
1 teaspoon kosher salt
1 teaspoon allspice
1½ pounds fresh green beans, stems removed and cu in half (frozen beans may be substituted)
1 (14.5-ounce) can peeled whole tomatoes, crushed o stewed tomatoes
½ cup pine nuts (optional)

Step 1:
Heat the oil in a saucepan. Add the onion and garlic and sauté until softened.

Step 2:
Add the meat; season with salt and allspice and sauté 10 to 15 minutes or until the meat is no longer pink and the mixture is dry.

Step 3:
Begin cooking Syrian rice (page 187 or 189).

Step 4:
Add the beans and tomatoes and cook (cover with lid tilted) 20 minutes longer or until the green beans are crisp tender. Add the pine nuts if desired and mix.

KABOB AND CHERRIES

Kabob Keddes *Yield: 6 to 7 servings*

Virginia's husband Tony, who is of Italian descent, teases our family about our method of cooking cherries or olives. Though he jokes about it, he never complains when he eats this meal or *jaj zatoon* (page 114). Mixing cherries with lamb may sound unusual, but after tasting this meal you will savor the combined flavors.

When serving, cut the pita into medium-size pieces. Put on a rimmed platter and top with some juice. Place the kabobs on the bread and add the cherries. The bread soaks up the juices and is really delicious. Garnish with pine nuts and parsley. You can eat as is or with Syrian rice on the side.

*2 pounds ground lamb (*kafta*)*
¼ cup chopped flat-leaf parsley (optional)
1 teaspoon kosher salt
1 teaspoon allspice
1 (16-ounce) cans dark sweet pitted cherries
1 teaspoon fresh lemon juice

Garnish
2 (6-inch) pita
¼ cup pine nuts
2 tablespoons chopped flat-leaf parsley

Step 1:

Mix the meat, parsley, salt and allspice in a bowl. Wrap a piece of meat around a skewer and mold into a finger-shape kabob, about 2-inches long and 1-inch wide. Slide the kabob off the skewer, and place in an ungreased pan. Broil for 5 minutes on each side until lightly browned. They should be slightly pink inside.

The kabobs can be prepared ahead of time and refrigerated uncooked. Broil ten minutes before dinner.

Continued

Step 2:

Begin cooking Syrian rice (page 187 or 189)

Step 3:

Fifteen minutes before dinner pour the cherries into a saucepan with 1 cup of juice from the can. Add the lemon juice and mix. Simmer (cover with lid tilted) on low heat 15 minutes or until heated through.

KABOB AND STUFFED LAMB MEATBALLS IN EGGPLANT GARLIC YOGURT

Alinazeek *Yield: 8 to 10 servings*

The preparation for *alinazeek*, which is characterized by its spicy yogurt base, is time consuming, but definitely worth the effort.

The eggplant, kabobs, *kibbeh* patties, yogurt (*leban*), and parsley can be prepared the day before serving; just reheat the kabobs and patties.

Kibbeh Nayeh

- *1 teaspoon kosher salt*
- *2 pounds leanest cut of ground lamb (*hubra*)*
- *1 1/2 cups #1 wheat*
- *1 medium yellow onion, grated*

Stuffing

- *1 1/2 pounds coarsely chopped (*mafroomah*) or ground (*kafta*) lamb*
- *1 medium yellow onion, minced*
- *1/2 cup pine nuts*
- *2 teaspoons da'ah (page 19)*
- *1 teaspoon kosher salt*

Kabobs

- *1 1/2 pounds ground lamb (*kafta*)*
- *1/4 cup chopped flat-leaf parsley*
- *1 1/2 teaspoons allspice*
- *1 teaspoon kosher salt*

Sauce

- *2 quarts plain yogurt*
- *2 large eggplants (2 pounds), broiled, skinned and mashed*
- *3 cloves garlic, minced*

Utensil
Skewer

Garnish
½ cup toasted pine nuts
¼ cup chopped flat-leaf parsley

Step 1:

Add 1 teaspoon salt to the meat and mix well. Refrigerate until ready to use. Place the wheat in a bowl and cover with cold water. Drain into a fine strainer; rinse again; drain and refrigerate for ½ hour.

Step 2:

Put the grated onion into the bowl containing the wheat. Add the meat and knead well, wetting your hands in cold water occasionally while mixing until you have a somewhat firm, smooth texture, and pleasing flavor. Taste and add additional salt and/or water if needed. Refrigerate.

Step 3:

Sauté the *mafroomah* or *kafta* on low/medium heat for 10 minutes. Add the onion and continue cooking until the meat is no longer pink and the mixture is fairly dry. Mix occasionally. This should take approximately 15 minutes. Mix in the pine nuts, *da'ah*, and 1 teaspoon salt. Set aside to cool.

Step 4:

Hold an egg-size piece of *kibbeh nayeh* and with your thumb, make a depression in it deep enough to accommodate 1 full tablespoon of stuffing. Seal and smooth out. Sitto Helen always keeps a small bowl of ice water next to her so she can wet her hands while smoothing out the *kibbeh* balls. Make sure they are completely closed and smooth, otherwis they may break open while cooking. You will have to roll them around in your hand a few times to do this. Slightly flatten each ball into the shap of a patty. Fill a deep pot with lightly salted water; bring to a boil and pu in the patties. Lower the heat and simmer for approximately 5 minutes. Pour gently into a colander and set aside.

Step 5:

Mix the *kafta* with the parsley, allspice, and 1 teaspoon salt and make small kabobs. To do this, take a small piece of meat, wrap it around a skewer and shape into a kabob, approximately 2-inches long and 1-inch wide. Slide off the skewer and place in an ungreased pan and broil 5 minutes on each side. They should be slightly pink inside. Set aside.

Step 6:

Put the yogurt in a pot; mix and simmer over low heat. Keep stirring for 15 minutes or until the yogurt gets hot. Add the eggplant and garlic and simmer for ½ hour. Stir occasionally.

Step 7:

When serving, pour the yogurt, garlic and eggplant mixture into a deep platter. Place the broiled kabobs over the mixture and garnish with pine nuts and parsley. Serve *kibbeh* patties on the side and enjoy!

LAMB AND ARTICHOKES

Riz ou Showky *Yield: 6 servings*

Made for artichoke lovers, this preparation capitalizes on the vegetable' unique flavor, which permeates the entire dish. We recommend fres artichokes, but frozen may be substituted. Syrian rice, garnished with pin nuts goes nicely with it and, of course, no Syrian meal would be complet without pita.

Riz ou showky can also be cooked without tomatoes. Add ¼ cup lemon juic and enough cold water to equal the amount of tomatoes in the recipe.

*8 medium artichokes or 2 (10-ounce) boxes frozen**
1 teaspoon lemon juice
1 tablespoon canola oil
1 cup chopped yellow onion
2 cloves garlic, minced
*1½ pounds ground (*kafta*) or cubed (*shish kabob*) lamb*
1 teaspoon kosher salt
1 teaspoon allspice
1 (14.5-ounce) can peeled whole, crushed, or stewed tomatoes
1 cup cold water

Step 1:

Rinse the artichokes and pat dry. Cut 1 inch off the top of each artichoke and approximately ½ inch off the stem (base). With a sharp knife, peel a thin piece of the outer layer from the stem. Remove all of the outer leave leaving the lighter, softer ones intact. Cut the artichokes in half lengthwise and, with the tip of a potato peeler or sharp utensil, remove the "thistle" or the hairy portion of the vegetable. Place the artichokes in col water and add the lemon juice to prevent them from turning black. Set aside.

* If using frozen artichokes, thaw and drain.

Step 2:

Begin cooking Syrian rice (page 187 or 189)

Step 3:

Pour the oil into a pan and heat. Add the onion and garlic and sauté until softened. Add the meat and season with salt and allspice. Mix and sauté for 10 to 15 minutes on low heat or until the meat is no longer pink. Drain excess juices and add the artichokes, tomatoes, and water. Mix, cover with lid tilted, and cook 30 minutes, or until the artichokes are tender.

LAMB BURGERS

Kabob *Yield: 6 to 7 burgers*

These specially seasoned burgers are succulent grilled and topped with ketchup or fresh, sliced tomato, served in either hamburger buns or pita. They can also be served plain with mashed potatoes and a Syrian salad on the side. Pour the burger juices over the potatoes when serving.

For non-Syrians the term "kabob" is now used to describe anything skewered and grilled whether vegetables, shrimp or meat. This should not be confused with *shish kabob*, the Armenian term for what Syrians call *mishwie* (skewered and grilled pieces of lamb).

*1½ pounds ground lamb (*kafta*)*
1 teaspoon allspice
1 medium yellow onion, minced
3 tablespoons chopped flat-leaf parsley
1 teaspoon dried mint (optional)
¼ cup pine nuts
1 teaspoon kosher salt
¼ cup ketchup (optional)
2 teaspoons Worcestershire sauce (optional)

Step 1:
In a bowl put the meat, allspice, onion, parsley, mint, nuts, salt, ketchup and Worcestershire sauce if desired. Mix well, and make individual patties.

Step 2:
Barbecue until slightly pink inside. Alternately, they may be broiled in the oven. The latter method preserves the juices.

LAMB CUTLETS

Shel'hath *Yield: 3 to 4 servings*

For a hot pita sandwich try these especially tender marinated cutlets. Philip enjoys them topped with ketchup.

They can also be served with a potato and/or vegetable and a Syrian salad.

1 pound lamb cutlets
3 tablespoons olive oil
1 tablespoon white vinegar
1 teaspoon allspice
½ teaspoon kosher salt

Step 1:
Pound cutlets with a mallet to tenderize, if desired. Pour the oil and vinegar into a bowl. Add the allspice, salt and mix. Pour over the cutlets and refrigerate overnight. Turn the cutlets over a few times while marinating.

Step 2:
Put the cutlets and marinade in an ungreased skillet, and sauté a few minutes on each side or broil or grill medium/rare.

LAMB MEATBALLS IN LEMON/TOMATO SAUCE

Da'oud Bacha *Yield: 3 to 4 servings*

This meal can be prepared beforehand and heated before serving. It is simple to make and quite flavorsome. Serve with Syrian rice.

2 slices white bread, crusts removed and discarded
2 tablespoons whole milk
*1 pound ground lamb (*kafta*)*
1 teaspoon allspice
½ teaspoon kosher salt
3 tablespoons chopped flat-leaf parsley
½ cup pine nuts or more if needed
Canola oil
Vegetable shortening
1 (8-ounce) box frozen peas

Sauce

1 (15-ounce) can peeled whole tomatoes, crushed
1 teaspoon sugar (optional)

Step 1:

Mix the bread with the milk. Add the meat, allspice, salt, and parsley and mix well. Hollow out a small meatball-size piece of meat with your thumb. Place 5 or 6 pine nuts into the opening and close. Smooth with slightly wet hands making sure the meatball is completely closed.

Step 2:

Cover the bottom of the frying pan with equal amounts of oil and shortening and heat. Fry the meatballs until lightly browned on all sides. Drain well on paper towels and set aside.*

*As an alternate method, the meatballs can be placed directly in the sauce without frying. Cook an additional 15 minutes.

Step 3:

Begin cooking Syrian rice (page 187 or 189).

Step 4:

Put the tomatoes and sugar into a pot and stir. Cover with lid tilted and bring to a slow boil. Add the meatballs, lower the heat, and simmer 30 minutes. Add the peas and continue cooking 5 minutes longer.

LAMB IN ROLLED FILLO

Sabegh Lahmeh *Yield: 50*

These tidbits are favorites for holiday entertaining! Though a bit delicate they hold together when made correctly. They can be served as an appe tizer or main dish with yogurt and a Syrian salad. The pomegranate molasse (*dibs rim'an*) adds zest.

The meat mixture can be prepared beforehand and refrigerated. Break up th mixture with a fork before using since it tends to harden after refrigeration.

If you intend to freeze the meat fingers, do not bake completely. When read to use, thaw and finish baking on a tray sprayed lightly with oil for 20 min utes or until heated through. You can also freeze them unbaked; just butte the tops first. Place waxed paper in between the layers when freezing.

This specialty is favored as a finger food.

*2 pounds ground lamb (*kafta*)*
2 large yellow onions, minced and squeezed tightly to remove excess water
½ cup pine nuts
¼ cup pomegranate molasses (page 185)
½ teaspoon white pepper
½ teaspoon allspice
1 teaspoon kosher salt
3 tablespoons fresh lemon juice
1 cup melted rendered butter (page 186)
1 pound #4 fillo dough, at room temperature

Step 1:
Lightly butter 2 rimmed baking pans (approximately 11 x 16 inches) and set aside.

Step 2:
Sauté the meat over medium/low heat for 10 minutes. Add the onions and continue cooking until the meat is no longer pink and the mixture is dry. Mix occasionally. Add the nuts, molasses, white pepper, allspice, salt, and lemon juice; mix well and set aside. Cool completely before using.

Step 3:
Preheat the oven to 350 degrees.

Step 4:
Place the dough on a cutting board and cut in half, parallel to the short side. Fold a sheet in half lengthwise. Place 1 tablespoon of *kafta* mixture on the sheet at the short end, spreading the meat out slightly. Brush the other end lightly with butter. Fold the sides of the fillo over the meat and carefully roll until completely sealed. Place seam side down in a pan. Repeat the process with the rest of the dough and meat. With a pastry brush, butter the tops of each roll, and bake 30 minutes or until golden brown on top and bottom. It is not necessary to turn them over.

LAMB TURNOVERS

Sambousak *Yield: 40 to 45*

These pastry turnovers can be baked or fried. They taste great either way. *Sambousak* is common to Indian cuisine as well, but differs somewhat in taste and texture. The allspice and pomegranate juice that gives it its tang distinguishes ours.

Serve with a Syrian salad or fresh vegetables and yogurt.

Sambousak can be frozen before cooking. To prepare for freezing, place in a pa or plastic container with waxed paper between each layer. Do not overlap. Cover tightly.

*1 1/2 pounds ground lamb (*kafta*)*
1 cup chopped yellow onion
1 teaspoon kosher salt
1/2 teaspoon white pepper
1 teaspoon allspice
*1/2 cup chopped walnuts or 1/2 cup pine nuts**
4 tablespoons fresh lemon juice
5 tablespoons pomegranate molasses (page 185)

**Walnuts and pine nuts can be used together (1/4 cup of each).*

Dough
7 cups all-purpose flour
1 1/2 cups warm water
2 cups vegetable shortening, melted

Vegetable shortening for frying
Canola oil for frying

Step 1:

Put the meat in a skillet and sauté 10 minutes. Add the onions and continue cooking until the meat is no longer pink and juices are absorbed. Transfer to a bowl and add the salt, white pepper, allspice, walnuts, and/or pine nuts. Add the lemon juice and molasses. Mix and set aside to cool.

Remember, the amount of spices and liquids can vary by individual tastes! It is your personal choice!

Step 2:

Put the flour and water in a long pan and mix with your hands. Add the 2 cups melted shortening. Do not knead. Pat the mixture back and forth using the palms of your hands and turn the dough repeatedly until thoroughly mixed. Use the dough as soon as possible so it does not dry out. Keep it in a covered pot or bowl while you are making the turnovers. Though the dough may feel tough, the turnovers will be quite flaky when cooked.

Step 3:

Take an egg-size piece of dough and with a rolling pin spread into a circle approximately 4 inches in diameter. Place 1 tablespoon of meat stuffing in the center of the dough and fold one side over to the other side. Pinch together with your fingers to seal the opening. Press fork tines down around the edges for a fancy effect.

Step 4:

a) **BAKING**: Preheat the oven to 350 degrees. Coat two trays with 3 to 4 tablespoons of melted shortening. Two trays should be sufficient, but if you need another tray repeat the process. Place the turnovers on the trays and bake 25 to 30 minutes or until golden brown, turning once. Serve warm.

b) **FRYING**: Pour an equal amount of melted shortening and canola oil into a wide, deep pan. Oil and shortening should be at least ½ inch deep. Fry the turnovers until golden brown on both sides. Drain well on paper towels. Serve warm.

MEAT PIES

Lahem'ajeen *Yield: 80 to 90*

Watch these Syrian mini-pizzas carefully because everyone loves ther Sitto Helen's grandchildren go wild over them and they disappear quic ly. Initially Sitto Helen used allspice but now prefers white pepper. If you a her why, she just shrugs and does not reply. Virginia recommends both.

We indicate 4 pounds of meat, but the recipe can be halved. Remember th it is always wiser to make more than less, especially when you have a lar family. These pies are wonderful frozen standbys when relatives or frien stop by unexpectedly. They do not take long to thaw and you just pop the into an oven or toaster oven for 10 minutes or until heated through.

Meat pies are delicious sprinkled lightly with dried mint and served wi yogurt and fresh vegetables. They can also be served as an appetizer; ju make them smaller.

In the souks of Aleppo, *lahem'ajeen* is very large and served rolled up as sandwich wrapped in waxed paper.

Dough

4 pounds (12 cups) all-purpose flour
1 packet active dry yeast
½ cup olive oil
1½ teaspoons salt
¾ cup melted vegetable shortening
4 cups warm water

Filling

*4 pounds ground lamb (*kafta*)*
2 pounds yellow onions, minced and squeezed tightl a few times to remove excess juices
¾ cup fresh or bottled lemon juice
1 (8-ounce) can tomato sauce
¾ cup dried mint
2 tablespoons kosher salt
1 tablespoon allspice
1 tablespoon white pepper

2 cups pomegranate molasses (page 185)
1 cup pine nuts
2 large red or green bell peppers, minced (optional)
3 cups all-vegetable shortening, melted or more if needed

Step 1:
Put the flour, yeast, oil, salt, and shortening in a large, deep bowl. Mix, and add the water slowly until the dough is thoroughly blended and relatively dry. Cover the bowl with a heavy cloth or towel and set aside for 2 hours in a warm place. Dough will rise slightly.

Step 2:
Put the meat, onions, lemon juice, tomato sauce, mint, salt, allspice, white pepper, molasses, pine nuts, and peppers (optional) into a large bowl and mix well. Cover and refrigerate.

Step 3:
Lay out sheets of waxed paper on a work surface and sprinkle with flour. Also, sprinkle flour on the palms of your hands so the dough does not stick to them. Roll pieces of dough into balls 2 inches in diameter and place on the work surface. When the dough is finished, cover with a light colored cloth, and let rest 1 hour.

Step 4:
Preheat the oven to 350 degrees.

Step 5:
Grease each of 3 large baking pans with ¼ cup of melted shortening or enough to coat the bottom of the pans. Add additional shortening to coat the bottom of the pans before making each batch of meat pies.

Place a dough ball in the pan and flatten into a circle approximately 4 inches in diameter. Six should fit in each pan. Put approximately three tablespoons of meat filling on the dough, spreading the meat with your hands almost to the edge. Flatten slightly. Mix the filling often to keep the juices evenly distributed.

Bake until the bottoms and edges are lightly browned. This should take 30 to 35 minutes. If you feel the meat pies are not cooking fast enough raise the temperature to 400 degrees.

SAUSAGE

Sau'seejaw and Simaneth *Yield: 3 to 4 servings*

Syrian sausage comes in two varieties: a thin version stuffed with mea pine nuts and spices, *sau'seejaw*, and the wider *simaneth* stuffed wi meat, chickpeas, rice and spices.

Sau'seejaw

If you prefer not making them yourself (and you are lucky enough to live New Jersey), you can purchase these sausages from George's Meat Marke Getty Avenue, Paterson, New Jersey. His are as authentic as they come. Gre as an appetizer or entrée, these sausages can be either grilled, pan fried broiled and served unadorned. They can also be broiled and then cooked tomato sauce and lemon juice. Serve either version with mashed potatoes, Syrian salad, and pita. You will double your pleasure if you pour the juices ov the potatoes.

The sausage casings can be purchased from most Middle Eastern markets ar refrigerated indefinitely in a closed container filled with kosher salt.

2 to 3 sheep casings
1 teaspoon lemon juice
*1 pound ground lamb (*kafta*)*
½ teaspoon da'ah (page 19)
½ teaspoon kosher salt
¼ cup pine nuts
1 cup tomato sauce (optional)
¼ cup lemon juice (optional)

Utensil
Meat-stuffing funnel with small/medium aperture or an electric mixer with stuffing attachment.

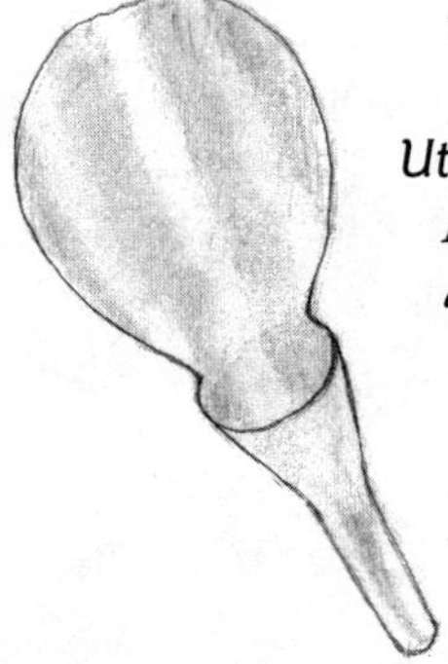

ep 1:

Remove casings from jar and soap lightly with your hands. Rinse thoroughly. Soak in cold water and 1 teaspoon of lemon juice overnight.

ep 2:

In a bowl, mix well the meat, *da'ah*, salt, and nuts.

ep 3:

Remove a casing from the water. Open one end with your fingers and blow into it. Securely stand the utensil on its wide end and slip the casing over the funnel opening. Leave a few inches at the end or tie a knot. If you use a stuffing attachment on an electric mixer, follow the directions accordingly.

ep 4:

Hold the funnel over a platter. Place a handful of meat in it and with your thumb push the meat through slowly until all the casing is filled. You may have to manually nudge the casing along as it fills with meat so it does not rip.

ep 5:

When finished, massage the sausage with your hand so it is the same diameter throughout its length. Lift it in the middle and form a double braid by twisting the parallel sections together every 2½ inches. Knot the ends.

ep 6:

Broil the sausage 5 to 7 minutes on each side or grill on a low flame. The sausage can also be simmered in a mixture of 1 cup tomato sauce, ¼ cup lemon juice and 1 cup water for approximately 20 minutes. When finished cooking, separate each sausage link from one another.

If serving as a cocktail party appetizer, simply heat in lemon juice and keep warm in a chafing dish.

maneth on following page

Simaneth

2 to 3 hog casings
Peel of 1 small lemon, cut up
Peel of 1 small orange, cut up
*1 pound coarsely chopped lamb (*mafroomah*)*
1 cup chickpeas, skins removed
½ teaspoon da'ah (page 19)
½ teaspoon kosher salt
½ cup uncooked white rice

Utensil

Meat-stuffing funnel with very large aperture

Step 1:

Soap the casings lightly with your hands, and rinse thoroughly. Turn inside out and carefully scrape off any visible fat with a sharp, non-serrated knife. Turn back. Refrigerate overnight in a bowl of cold water, and the cut-up peels of the lemon and orange.

Step 2:

In a bowl, mix well the meat, chickpeas, *da'ah*, salt, and rice.

Step 3:

Remove a casing from the water. Open one end with your fingers. Securely stand the utensil on its wide end and slip the casing over the funnel opening. Leave a few inches at the end or tie a knot. Place a handful of meat mixture in it and with your thumb push through slowly until all the casing is filled. You may have to nudge the casing along as it fills so it does not rip. If you use a stuffing attachment on an electric mixer, follow the directions accordingly.

When finished, massage the sausage with your hand so it is the same diameter throughout its length. Then flatten to approximately 1-inch thick. Lift each sausage strand in the middle, twist to divide in half and form a double braid. Twist the parallel sections together every 3 inches. With a fork, pierce each sausage link three times. Knot the ends.

Step 4:

Put the sausage in a pot and cover with cold water. Bring to a boil, lower the flame and simmer 45 minutes. Remove the sausage and reserve the water. Use the water to cook *burghol* (page 181), which can be served as a side dish with yogurt.

SHISH KABOB

Mishwie *Yield: 3 to 4 servings*

f you like to barbecue, you will love this, the most recognized Middle Eastern dish in America. Needless to say, it is convenient, easy to prepare ıd great for parties or picnics. It makes a perfect sandwich on pita and can be rved alone with a Syrian salad or with a vegetable and potato or Syrian rice age 187 or 189).

1 pound prime lamb, cubed
¼ cup olive oil
2 tablespoons white vinegar
½ teaspoon kosher salt
1 teaspoon allspice
5 small white onions
1 red or green bell pepper, cut into wide slices
5 cherry tomatoes
5 large whole mushrooms, stems removed
2 (6-inch) or 1 large pita, split and separated

ep 1:
In a bowl, mix the meat, oil, vinegar, salt, and allspice. The mixture should be slightly tart. Marinate a few hours or overnight in the refrigerator, mixing occasionally.

ep 2:
Put the meat, onions, peppers, tomatoes, and mushrooms onto skewers in alternating sequence and barbecue or broil to medium rare.

To serve, cut pita in half, separate the top from the bottom and place in a bowl. Put the meat and vegetables on the bottom half of the bread and cover with the top. The juices from the meat add a unique flavor to the bread.

RMENIAN VERSION: George Hayek and his sons, our butchers in Paterson, New Jersey, prepare hundreds of pounds of *shish kabob* for numerous Armenian festivals throughout the state each year. They marinate the meat overnight with coriander, black pepper, salt, lemon juice, sliced onion, paprika, and olive oil, and claim it is as fine as the Syrian version.

SPINACH PIES

Fatayer Sabinech *Yield: 60*

The most familiar version of this triangular spinach pie is of Greek origin. It made with fillo dough and stuffed with spinach, feta and/or cottage chees eggs, scallions, onions and spices. Our recipe is made with plain dough, and stuffed with spinach, parsley, onions, nuts, and spices. The texture and flavor each are quite different, but equally tasty. Recipe can be halved.

Dough

1 packet active dry yeast
3½ cups warm water
4 pounds (12 cups) all-purpose flour
½ cup olive oil
1½ teaspoons kosher salt

Stuffing

7 (10-ounce) boxes frozen chopped spinach or 5 pounds fresh spinach
3 cups chopped flat-leaf parsley
4 large yellow onions, minced (approximately 2 cu
½ cup olive oil
1 cup shelled walnuts, chopped medium
1¼ cups fresh or bottled lemon juice
1 cup pine nuts
1 tablespoon allspice
1 tablespoon white pepper
1 tablespoon kosher salt
Canola oil

Step 1:

Dissolve yeast in the warm water and mix well. Set aside.

Mix the flour, ½ cup oil, and salt in a large bowl. Gradually add the yeast/water mixture. Knead well for 5 minutes or until the dough is well blended. The dough will be slightly dry. Cover the bowl with a heavy cloth or towel, and set aside in a warm place for 2 hours.

Step 2:
If using frozen spinach, thaw and squeeze tightly a few times to remove excess water. If using fresh spinach, discard the stems and rinse well. Steam until tender; cool, and chop fine. Squeeze liquid from minced onions as well and mix with the spinach. It is important to remove as much liquid as possible from the spinach and onions. Set aside.

Step 3:
Place sheets of waxed paper on work surface and sprinkle with flour. Also, sprinkle your hands with flour so the dough does not stick to them. Form a ball with a meatball-size piece of dough in the palms of your hands. Place it on the paper. When completely finished, cover the dough with a light-colored cloth or large towel. Set aside for one hour.

Step 4:
In a bowl, mix well the spinach, parsley, onions, oil, walnuts, lemon juice, pine nuts, allspice, white pepper, and salt. The mixture should taste tart. Add more spices and lemon juice if needed.

Step 5:
Preheat oven to 350 degrees.

You may need 2 or 3 large baking pans to accommodate all the pies. Coat each pan with canola oil. Additional oil must be added to the pans before making each batch of spinach pies.

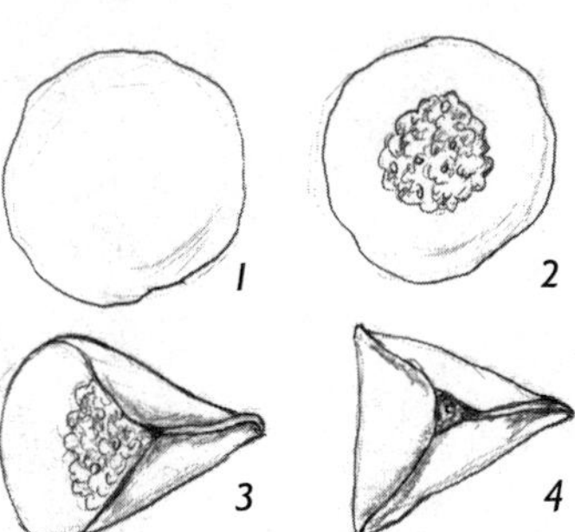

With a rolling pin, flatten a dough ball into a circle 5 inches in diameter and place approximately 2 tablespoons of spinach mixture in the center. Visualize a triangle in the circle and fold the edges of the circle up to form a pyramid, with a pea-size opening in the top. To do this, pull up 2 edges of the circle (⅓ of the dough) and pinch together. Pull up the remaining ⅔ of the dough (from the middle), and pinch it to the other edges, leaving a small opening in the middle. Place in the pan and bake for 40 to 45 minutes or until golden brown on top and bottom.

Serve as an appetizer or main meal with yogurt and fresh vegetables. If you freeze the pies, thaw them and heat in a moderate oven for 5 to 10 minutes or until heated through.

SQUASH STUFFED WITH LAMB AND RICE IN TOMATO LEMON SAUCE

Coussa Mahshee *Yield: 8 to 10 servings*

Any summer squash, white, green, or yellow is ideal for stuffing. Red or green bell peppers, potatoes and tomatoes can also be filled with our seasoned meat rice mixture. Virginia's husband, Tony, prefers stuffed potatoes instead of squash so a potato is always added to the pot. He says any type will do. Potatoes are a bit harder to scoop out, but well worth the effort. Just ask Tony!

To stuff a potato, scrub well, pat dry and stand on end (do not peel). Cut a small piece off the top and scoop out the insides, leaving about ½ inch of potato innards. Stuff with filling.

Peppers and tomatoes are prepared in the same fashion. We recommend placing them on top of the squash and/or potatoes since they cook faster.

6 pounds squash (about 14), approximately 6-inches long and 2½ inches in diameter
7 or 8 lamb bones (optional)

Stuffing
*2 pounds coarsely chopped lamb (*mafroomah*)*
1¼ cups uncooked white rice
1 (8-ounce) can tomato sauce
2 teaspoons allspice
1 teaspoon kosher salt
¼ cup cold water

Sauce
1 (28-ounce) can peeled whole tomatoes, crushed
2 cups fresh or bottled lemon juice
¼ cup dried mint
1 head or 10 cloves garlic, crushed
1 teaspoon kosher salt

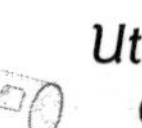

Utensils
Coring tool
Long scraping tool

Step 1:

Scrub the squash with a vegetable brush and rinse under cold water. Set aside to drain or pat dry with paper towels. Cut approximately 1 inch, including the stem, off the top of the squash or other vegetables and discard. To give the squash a fancier look, we lightly scrape alternate strips of the outside skin with a vegetable peeler.

With the coring tool, hollow out the vegetables, being careful not to break through the sides or bottom. If you do break through, and some of the meat comes out while stuffing, tie the vegetable with string around the wound. Do not discard the innards from the squash. They can be cooked in the sauce and served on the side. You can also use them in an omelet.

Step 2:

Mix the meat, rice, tomato sauce, allspice, salt, and water.

Step 3:

Mix the tomatoes, lemon juice, mint, garlic, salt and set aside.

Step 4:

Stuff each vegetable, pushing down lightly with your fingers. Tap the bottom of the vegetable in the palm of your hand so the stuffing falls to the bottom more easily.

Step 5:

If using lamb bones, place them in a wide, deep pot, then place the squash upright on top of them starting in a circle and working around to the middle. Pour the sauce over the vegetables and place an inverted dish on top to prevent shifting. Cover the pot. Bring to a boil, lower the heat, and simmer 50 to 60 minutes. Taste a forkful of stuffing from one of the vegetables to see if the rice is cooked. Also, push fork tines into the squash to check for tenderness. If the vegetable or rice is still hard, continue cooking until tender. When the vegetables and rice are cooked, close the heat, tilt the cover, and pour the juices into a bowl. Use the juices to reheat leftovers. Recover the pot and let stand 15 minutes. Carefully remove the squash; place on a platter and serve.

Serve with yogurt and pita. Our custom is to open the squash along the top and to spoon some sauce and/or yogurt into it. It is delicious this way; just ask Virginia's niece Donna. She will not eat it any other way.

SQUASH STUFFED WITH LAMB AND RICE IN YOGURT

Coussa ou Leban *Yield: 8 to 10 servings*

This is another version of stuffed squash given to us by our cousin Marilyn. The title describes it pretty well and you will enjoy it if you like yogurt (*leban*). Preparation of the squash is the same as *coussa mahshee*, but it is cooked in yogurt rather than a tomato, lemon sauce.

6 pounds squash (about 14), approximately 6-inches long, and 2½ inches in diameter

Stuffing

*2 pounds coarsely chopped lamb (*mafroomah*)*
1¼ cups uncooked white rice
2 teaspoons allspice
1 teaspoon kosher salt
¼ cup cold water

Sauce

3 tablespoons cornstarch
½ cup cold water
2 quarts plain yogurt (whole or low fat)
2 eggs, beaten
8 cloves garlic, crushed
2 tablespoons dried mint
1 teaspoon kosher salt

Utensils

Coring tool
Long scraping tool

Step 1:

Scrub the squash with a vegetable brush and rinse under cold water. Set aside to drain or pat dry with paper towels. Cut approximately 1 inch, including the stem, off the top of the squash and discard.

With the coring tool (round cylinder) hollow out the vegetables, being careful not to break through the sides or bottom. Insert the scraper and clean out as much of the innards as possible. If you do break through, and some of the meat comes out while stuffing, tie the vegetable with string around the wound. Do not discard the innards from the squash. They can be cooked in the sauce and served on the side. You can also use them in an omelet.

Step 2:

Mix the meat, rice, allspice, salt and water.

Step 3:

Stuff each vegetable, pushing down lightly with your fingers. Tap the bottom of the vegetable in the palm of your hand so the stuffing falls to the bottom more easily.

Step 4:

Dissolve the cornstarch in the water and mix well. Put the yogurt in a wide, deep pot; add the cornstarch and water mixture and mix. Add the eggs and mix again. On low to medium heat, bring to a boil while continuously stirring. Lower the heat and simmer two minutes to thicken. Mix in the garlic, mint, and salt. Place each squash in the yogurt mixture one at a time. Place an inverted dish on top to prevent shifting. Do not cover the pot. Simmer on low heat for 50 minutes or until the squash and rice are tender.

When serving, place the squash on a dish and cover with cooked yogurt. Serve with pita and fresh vegetables.

STUFFED CABBAGE IN TANGY SAUCE

Lekhanah *Yield: 8 to 10 servings*

Though considered an "international" dish, its unusual seasonings distinguish our stuffed cabbage. Pomegranate molasses (*dibs rim'an*) and mint add a unique flavor, and lamb, of course, has a sweet flavor all its own.

Serve with raw vegetables and pita. Yogurt makes for a cooling contrast.

2-medium size light density cabbage heads (6 pounds total)
8 lamb bones (optional)

Stuffing

2 pounds coarsely ground lamb (mafroomah)
1¼ cups uncooked white rice
1 (8-ounce) can tomato sauce
2 teaspoons allspice
¼ cup cold water
1 teaspoon kosher salt

Sauce

1 (28-ounce) can peeled whole tomatoes, crushed
2 cups fresh or bottled lemon juice
¼ cup dried mint
1 head or 10 cloves garlic, crushed
2 tablespoons pomegranate molasses (page 185)
1 teaspoon kosher salt

Step 1:

Rinse the cabbage and discard any blemished leaves. Cut across the base so the outer leaves separate slightly from the core. With a paring knife, remove as much of the core as possible. Carefully place the cabbage into boiling water and lower the heat. Slow boil, and as the leaves loosen, remove and place in a colander to drain. The whole process should take approximately 25 minutes. If refrigerating for later use, place a few paper towels in the bottom of a pan with the leaves on top to absorb excess water.

Step 2:

Mix the meat, rice, sauce, allspice, water, salt and set aside.

Step 3:

Mix the tomatoes, lemon juice, mint, garlic, molasses, salt and set aside.

Step 4:

Place a cabbage leaf on a cutting board "rib" side up. Slice off the top of the rib if it seems too thick. Turn the leaf over. If the leaf is very large cut it in half lengthwise and discard the rib portion. Put approximately two tablespoons of stuffing lengthwise along the widest edge of the leaf and roll into the shape of a cigar. Do not fold in the sides. Leave ½ inch of unfilled leaf at each end.

Step 5:

If you have lamb bones, put them in a wide, deep pot and layer the stuffed cabbage leaves over them starting with the darker/tougher outer leaves. Pour the sauce over the cabbage and place an inverted dish on top to prevent shifting. Cover the pot and bring the liquid to a full boil. Lower the heat and simmer 45 to 50 minutes. Before turning off the heat, remove a cabbage roll and taste to make sure the rice and vegetables are cooked thoroughly. When completely cooked, close the heat, tilt the cover, and pour the juices into a bowl. Use the juices to reheat leftovers. Recover the pot and let stand 15 minutes. Carefully remove the cabbage; place on a platter and serve.

SYRIAN MEATLOAF

Yield: 4 to 5 servings

Consider this an American favorite with a Syrian touch. It is as easy to prepare as the basic American beef recipe, but we have substituted lamb and added allspice for contrast. Serve with potatoes, a vegetable, salad, and pita.

Leftovers are great in sandwiches.

*1 pound ground lamb (*kafta*)*
1 extra-large egg, beaten
2 cloves garlic, minced
1 medium yellow onion, minced
1 small green or red bell pepper, minced
3 tablespoons chopped flat-leaf parsley
½ cup plain bread crumbs
¼ cup ketchup
2 teaspoons Worcestershire sauce
½ teaspoon kosher salt
1 teaspoon allspice
6 or 7 small red potatoes, parboiled
1 (8-ounce) can tomato sauce
1 cup cold water

Step 1:
Preheat the oven to 350 degrees.

Step 2:
Put the meat, egg, garlic, onion, pepper, parsley, bread crumbs, ketchup, Worcestershire sauce, salt, and allspice in a bowl and mix well. Shape into a loaf and smooth evenly. Place in a baking pan surrounded by the potatoes.

Step 3:
Mix the tomato sauce with the water and pour over the loaf and potatoes. Bake for 1¼ hours or until the meat is no longer pink inside. Baste occasionally. If the tomato mixture evaporates, add more water.

SYRIAN TURKEY BURGERS

Yield: 4 to 5 servings

Unlike the conventional beef or lamb burger this one offers "lite" fare, and is tasty too! It is easy to prepare and tastes great grilled. You can top with a condiment of your choice, or just eat plain.

Serve on pita or a hamburger bun with a Syrian pickle on the side and one of our special potato salads.

3/4 cup cold water
1/8 cup #4 wheat
10 ounces lean ground turkey
3/4 cup fresh tomatoes, minced
1/4 cup scallions, minced
1/4 cup plain yogurt
2 teaspoons dried or fresh mint, minced
1/4 teaspoon cumin
1/4 teaspoon allspice
1/4 teaspoon kosher salt
4 wheat or plain pitas, split

Step 1:
Spray the grill or pan with cooking oil.

Step 2:
Bring the water to a boil in a small covered pot. Add the wheat, mix and recover. Simmer 25 minutes or until the wheat is tender and the water has evaporated. If the water evaporates too soon, add more. Set aside to cool.

Step 3:
In a bowl, mix well the wheat, turkey, tomatoes, scallions, yogurt, mint, cumin, allspice, and salt. Lightly moisten hands and shape into patties. Grill on medium heat for approximately 5 minutes on each side or until no longer pink inside.

TURKEY STEW

Jaj ou Bazala *Yield: 3 to 4 servings*

This is a good way to use up leftover turkey from Thanksgiving dinner. It i simple to prepare and yummy served over Syrian rice.

You can also substitute chicken for turkey if you like. It is scrumptious wit pita.

1 (14.5-ounce) can stewed or peeled whole tomatoes, crushed
1 cup chicken broth
3 tablespoons fresh or bottled lemon juice
2 cups cubed, cooked turkey (preferably white meat)
1 teaspoon kosher salt
½ teaspoon allspice
1 teaspoon sugar
1 (15-ounce) can peas, drained or 1 frozen package
1 tablespoon salted butter (optional)

Step 1:
Begin cooking Syrian rice (page 187 or 189)

Step 2:
Pour tomatoes, broth, and lemon juice into a saucepan. Mix well, cover with lid tilted, and bring to a slow boil. Lower the heat and simmer for 2 minutes.

Step 3:
Mix in the turkey, salt, allspice, and sugar. Simmer a few minutes longer. Add the peas and butter (optional) and cook until the peas are heated through. If you use frozen peas, you may have to simmer a few minutes longer.

Vegetarian Dishes

(Kuthra)

EGG AND PARSLEY PATTIES

Ir'jeh *Yield: 30 patties or 12 squares*

Ir'jeh, served in pita, topped with lettuce and eaten with fresh tomatoes, is a refreshing sandwich. Delicious with Sitto Helen's garlic pickles (page 59). This was our parents' favorite picnic food. It is easy to make, not messy and a great lunch to take on long trips. During the summer months, our families often stopped on the side of the road during the long trips to the "Jerro compound" in Tannersville, New York, located in the Catskill Mountains. We feasted on *Ir'jeh* sandwiches, garlic pickles, Syrian cheese, and Syrian cookies and loved every minute of it!

The exact same thing happens in Syria when your driver/guide pulls over to he side of the road, takes out a tablecloth, and treats you to lunch.

r'jeh also makes a tasty addition to any *mezze* tray. For an attractive presen-ation serve on a bed of lettuce surrounded by tomato wedges.

10 jumbo eggs
1½ cups chopped flat-leaf parsley
1 cup minced yellow onions, squeezed tightly to remove excess liquid
2 large cloves garlic, minced
1 tablespoon allspice
¼ cup dried mint
½ teaspoon kosher salt
Canola oil

Utensil

Heavy-duty pan with cavities similar to a poached egg pan. Called ir'jeh *pans, they can be purchased at most Middle Eastern markets. Try to find pans with deep cavities.*

tep 1:

Whisk the eggs in a large bowl. Add the parsley, onions, garlic, allspice, mint, salt, and mix well. The consistency should be thick.

Continued

Step 2:

Pour approximately 1 tablespoon of oil into each cavity of the pan and heat. Add 2 tablespoons egg mixture or enough to fill each cavity. Fry 3 minutes on each side or until nicely browned. Remove and drain well on paper towels.

Ir'jeh can also be baked in the oven. Use a 9 x 2-inch square pan; coat the bottom with 5 tablespoons of canola oil then pour the egg mixture in. Bake in a preheated 350 degree oven for 30 minutes or until lightly browned on top. Let cool and cut into 2 x 2-inch squares before serving.

EGGPLANT

Bantenjan *Yield: 5 servings*

There are several variations for cooking eggplant. They are equally tasty and easy to prepare.

Plain, fried eggplant makes for a perfect snack or picnic food in pita. For a tasty alternative, top with yogurt and/or lettuce. Delicious with Sitto Helen's famous garlic pickles (page 59).

Eggplant cooked with tomatoes or topped with yogurt can be served as a side dish with any grilled fish or meat entrée. Just scoop it up with pita.

Bantenjan Bana'doora

(eggplant cooked with tomatoes)

1 medium eggplant (1 pound)
3 tablespoons olive oil
1 large yellow onion, diced
1 cup diced fresh or canned tomatoes
½ teaspoon allspice
1 teaspoon kosher salt

Step 1:
Rinse the eggplant and pat dry. Cut off the stem, cut into medium-size cubes and set aside.

Step 2:
Heat the oil in a saucepan. Add the onion and sauté until soft. Add the eggplant, tomatoes, allspice and salt. Mix; cover with lid tilted and simmer 20 minutes or until the vegetable is tender.

Bantenjan Leban on following page

Bantenjan Leban

(fried eggplant topped with yogurt) *Yield: 14 servings*

2 medium-size eggplants (2 pounds)
Kosher salt
Canola oil
3 cloves garlic
2 to 3 cups yogurt (whole or low-fat)

Step 1:

Rinse the eggplants and pat dry. Cut off the stem; do not peel. Cut into ½-inch slices. Sprinkle lightly with salt and layer on a platter with paper towels in between. Press to absorb the excess moisture.

Step 2:

Pour enough oil into a skillet to coat the bottom and heat. Fry the slices until golden brown on both sides and place on paper towels to drain. Add additional oil as needed.

Step 3:

Crush the garlic with ½ teaspoon salt; add to the yogurt and mix. Place the eggplant slices in a deep dish or platter and cover with the yogurt mixture.

(Eggplant fried this way can also be eaten without yogurt or garlic. Just make a pita sandwich and sprinkle lightly with salt.)

Bantenjan Mitlee

(eggplant breaded and fried) *Yield: 5 to 6 pita servings*

1 large eggplant (1½ pounds)
Kosher salt
3 extra-large eggs
1 teaspoon whole milk
1½ cups seasoned bread crumbs
Canola oil

Step 1:

Rinse the eggplants and pat dry. Cut off the stem. Cut into ½-inch slices. Sprinkle lightly with salt and layer on a platter with paper towels in between. Press so the towels will absorb the excess moisture.

Step 2:

Beat the eggs in a bowl. Mix in the milk. Dip each slice of eggplant in the egg/milk mixture and then into the breadcrumbs.

Step 3:

Pour enough oil into a large skillet to coat the bottom and heat. Fry the eggplant until golden brown on both sides. Add more oil as needed. Drain well on paper towels.

Serve as pita sandwiches.

Variation on following page

Bantenjan Mitlee

(eggplant cooked in tomato sauce) *Yield: 6 servings*

Joe Kassis, our cousin Rita's husband, eats this with pita and watermelon. It sounds interesting and we recommend trying it this way if you feel daring. A lot of Syrians enjoy it on Ritz and other crackers.

1 large eggplant (1½ pounds)
Kosher salt
Canola oil
1 medium yellow onion, sliced
1 tablespoon tomato paste
1 (8-ounce) can tomato sauce
¼ teaspoon allspice
¼ teaspoon cumin

Step 1:

Rinse the eggplant and pat dry. Cut off the stem; do not peel. Cut into ½-inch slices or cubes. Sprinkle lightly with salt and layer on a platter with paper towels in between. Press to absorb the excess moisture.

Step 2:

Pour enough oil into a skillet to coat the bottom and heat. Fry the eggplant until golden brown on both sides. Add additional oil as needed. Remove and drain well on paper towels. When you are finished frying, discard all but 2 tablespoons of oil.

Step 3:

Add the onion to the pan and sauté until translucent. Add the eggplant, tomato paste, tomato sauce, ¼ teaspoon salt, allspice, and cumin. Mix; cover with lid tilted and bring to a slow boil. Lower the heat and simmer for 20 minutes. Refrigerate before serving.

FAVA BEANS WITH GARLIC

Foul em Demas *Yield: 2 servings*

This is a pleasant side dish with any grilled fish or meat entrée and can be served hot or cold as an appetizer with, of course, pita.

Serve garnished with tomato, parsley and, if you wish, a dab of yogurt.

2 tablespoons olive oil
1 large clove garlic, minced
1 teaspoon coriander
2 tablespoons fresh lemon juice
1/4 cup yellow onion, minced
1/2 teaspoon kosher salt
1/4 teaspoon allspice
1 (15-ounce) can fava beans

Garnish
1 medium tomato, minced
2 tablespoons chopped flat-leaf parsley
1 teaspoon plain yogurt (optional)

Step 1:
Heat 1 tablespoon olive oil in a skillet. Add the garlic and sauté 2 minutes. Add the coriander, mix, and simmer 2 minutes.

Step 2:
Mix the lemon juice, remaining oil, onion, garlic mixture, salt and allspice. Set aside.

Step 3:
Simmer the beans in a covered saucepan until heated through or heat briefly in a microwave oven. Drain and put them in a bowl. Pour the marinade over them. Mix before serving.

Can be served warm or cold.

FRIED CAULIFLOWER

Zahrah *Yield: 5 to 6 pita sandwiches*

Fried cauliflower, with a dab of yogurt and/or lettuce, makes a wonderful vegetarian sandwich in pita. It goes especially well with Sitto Helen's garlic pickles (page 59).

If you prefer a lighter version, parboil the florets then drain. Pat dry, place in a shallow pan lightly coated with canola oil and broil a few minutes on each side until golden brown. You can also fry the cauliflower plain.

1 head cauliflower (about 2 pounds)
3 extra-large eggs
½ teaspoon kosher salt
1 teaspoon whole milk
1½ cups seasoned bread crumbs
Canola oil

Step 1:
Rinse the cauliflower and separate the florets. Discard the stem and outer leaves. Parboil the florets for 3 minutes. Drain in a colander.

Step 2:
In a bowl, beat well the eggs, salt and milk. Dip each piece of cauliflower into the mixture and then into the breadcrumbs. Place on a platter.

Step 3:
Pour enough oil into a skillet to coat the bottom. Fry the cauliflower until golden brown on both sides. Drain well on paper towels.

FRIED SQUASH IN GARLIC VINEGAR

Coussa Mitlee *Yield: 3 to 4 servings*

When Sitto Alice visited her sister Helen and her family at their summer home, she prepared and cooked this cooling and special treat for her nieces, Virginia and Annette. They loved it and, like most aunts, it made her happy to please them. It is very simple to prepare, just a little time consuming because of the frying.

It is also a bit challenging to eat because the vinegar makes the pita soft, the juices drip out and the taste is quite tart. But that's what makes it so enjoyable. Delight in it as a lunch sandwich in pita.

1½ pounds green or yellow squash
Canola oil
¼ cup white vinegar
2 large cloves garlic, minced
½ teaspoon kosher salt

Step 1:
Rinse the squash, pat dry, and cut lengthwise into ½-inch slices. Cut again to approximately 3 inches in length.

Step 2:
Pour enough oil into a skillet to coat the bottom and heat. Fry the squash until golden brown on both sides. Place on paper towels to drain.

Step 3:
Mix the vinegar, garlic, and salt in a deep bowl. Add the squash; gently mix and set aside for 1 hour before serving.

GREEN BEANS IN TOMATO SAUCE

Fowleh ou Zath — *Yield: 4 servings*

This recipe can be prepared primarily as a vegetarian meal with *hummus*, *mou'jadara*, and pita or as a side dish with any fish or meat entrée.

2 pounds fresh green beans or
2 boxes frozen French-style green beans
½ cup yellow onion, minced
3 cloves garlic, minced
3 tablespoons olive oil
1 (14-ounce) can diced tomatoes or stewed tomatoes, crushed
½ cup cold water
1 teaspoon kosher salt
½ teaspoon allspice

Step 1:

Remove the stems from the fresh beans and cut in half or along the bean (French cut). Rinse well, drain, and set aside.

If using frozen beans, do not thaw, and do not add water when mixing with the tomatoes and spices as indicated in Step 3.

Step 2:

In a saucepan, sauté the onion and garlic in the oil for a few minutes unti softened.

Step 3:

Add the fresh or frozen beans, tomatoes, water, salt, and allspice. Bring the mixture to a boil and cover with lid tilted. Lower the heat and simmer 30 minutes or until the beans are tender/crisp. Do not overcook.

LENTIL AND WHEAT COMBO

Mou'jadara *Yield: 4 servings*

This Lenten staple is relatively easy to prepare and will bring out the delicious flavor of any lentil dish. Serve with *fowleh zath*, *hummus*, and pita.

½ cup olive oil
1 large yellow onion, thinly sliced
1 cup dry lentils
4 cups cold water (if wheat is used) or 3½ cups cold water (if rice is used)
2 chicken bouillon cubes (optional)
1 cup # 4 wheat or 1 cup uncooked white rice
1 teaspoon kosher salt

Step 1:

Heat the oil in a saucepan. Add the onion and sauté for 10 to 15 minutes or until nicely browned. Stir occasionally. Set aside.

Step 2:

Check lentils for small stones and discard. Rinse in a colander.

Step 3:

Boil the water in a wide, heavy pot, add the lentils and bouillon cubes if desired and cover. Reduce the heat and simmer for approximately 10 minutes. Add the wheat or rice and salt. Mix, recover, and cook for 30 to 35 minutes or until the lentils and grain are tender.

If the lentils and grain are not cooked and all the water has evaporated add another ¼ cup water or more if needed.

Step 4:

Pour the oil and onion over the lentils and grain. Mix and serve.

OKRA IN TOMATO SAUCE

Bameh *Yield: 4 to 5 servings*

This dish can be served as a side dish with any grilled fish or meat entrée. It can also be served alone with pita or over Syrian rice.

1 pound okra
3 tablespoons olive oil
½ cup yellow onion, minced
2 cloves garlic, minced
¼ cup fresh or bottled lemon juice
1 cup canned peeled whole tomatoes, crushed and mixed with 1 cup cold water, or 2 cups stewed tomatoes, crushed
1 tablespoon coriander
1 teaspoon allspice
1 teaspoon kosher salt
1 teaspoon sugar

Step 1:

Remove the stems from the fresh okra, rinse, and drain. Heat 2 tablespoons oil in a saucepan. Add the okra and sauté until tender and lightly browned. Remove from the pan and drain well on paper towels. Set aside.

If using frozen okra, thaw, and add to the pot as indicated in Step 2.

Step 2:

Begin preparing Syrian rice (page 187 or 189).

Step 3:

Add the remaining 1 tablespoon oil to the pan and heat. Add the onion and garlic and sauté until soft. Add the lemon juice, tomatoes, coriander, allspice, salt, and sugar. Mix well; cover with lid tilted and lower the heat Simmer 20 minutes or until thickened. Add the okra to the pot and mix lightly. Cook a few minutes longer or until the okra is heated through.

SPINACH IN GARLIC OIL

Sabanegh Hudra *Yield: 2 to 3 servings*

Serve as a side dish to any grilled meat or fish entrée or as a vegetarian meal with *hummus* and pita.

1 (10-ounce) package fresh spinach
1 tablespoon olive oil
1 small yellow onion, sliced thin
2 cloves garlic, minced
1 teaspoon coriander
½ teaspoon kosher salt

Utensil
Steamer

Step 1:
Remove the stems from the spinach, rinse well and drain. Shred the spinach into a pot with a steamer attachment, add water and cook 10 minutes or until softened. Drain through a colander. Set aside.

Step 2:
Put the oil, onion and garlic into a skillet and sauté a few minutes until softened and translucent.

Step 3:
Add the spinach, coriander, and salt. Mix and cook a few minutes longer until the spinach is heated through.

Side Dishes and Staples

CRACKED WHEAT SIDE DISH

Burghol *Yield: 4 servings as a side dish*

Burghol, simply enough, is cooked cracked wheat. It is easy to prepare and can be served as a side dish*, like rice, with any meat entrée. It can also be eaten alone with yogurt and pita on the side.

2¼ cups chicken broth
1 teaspoon kosher salt
½ teaspoon black pepper
1 cup #4 wheat
3 tablespoons salted butter

Step 1:
Boil the broth, salt, and pepper in a deep, wide covered pot.

Step 2:
Blend in the wheat and butter and lower the heat. Cover and simmer 25 to 30 minutes or until the wheat is tender and the broth has evaporated. If the broth evaporates and the wheat is still hard add additional broth (or water) as needed. Mix before serving.

*As a side dish for *dor'bough* (page 104), use water/vinegar mixture in the ratio of 2:1. For less tartness, use less vinegar and proportionately more water.

LAMB STUFFING

Hash'weh *Yield: 6 to 8 servings*

Although our family identifies this incredible blend of flavors as its trad tional turkey stuffing, it never actually gets inside the bird because it easier to cook separately. Removing all the stuffing from a turkey is usual impossible and it is a shame to waste any of this specialty.

Hash'weh makes a great side dish on Thanksgiving or with any poultry dinne Garnish with pomegranate seeds, toasted pine nuts and pistachios.

Leftover stuffing makes a fine breakfast or lunch sautéed in butter and scran bled with eggs. Serve with yogurt and pita.

You can also mix leftover stuffing, cooked fresh green beans, and stewed fresh diced tomatoes. Just combine to taste, heat through and serve ov Syrian rice (page 187 or 189) with pita.

*1½ pounds chopped lamb (*kafta *or* mafroomah*)*
1 medium yellow onion, minced
2½ cups chicken broth
¾ teaspoon kosher salt
1 cup uncooked white rice
2 teaspoons da'ah (page 19)
1 teaspoon cinnamon
¼ cup pine nuts
¼ cup pistachio nuts, skins removed

Garnish
½ cup pomegranate seeds
¼ cup pine nuts, lightly toasted
¼ cup pistachio nuts, skins removed

Step 1:
Sauté the meat in a large frying pan on low/medium heat for 10 minutes Add the onion and continue cooking until the meat is no longer pink an juices are absorbed (approximately 20 minutes).

Step 2:

Mix in the broth and salt, cover and bring to a boil. Add the rice and mix again. Recover and simmer for 30 to 35 minutes or until the broth is absorbed and the rice is tender. If the broth evaporates before the rice is cooked, add additional broth or water as needed.

Step 3:

Add the *da'ah*, cinnamon, plain pine nuts, ¼ cup pistachio nuts and mix. Place on a platter; top with pomegranate seeds, toasted pine nuts, additional pistachios, and serve.

PITA CHIPS

Yield: 48 to 64 chips

Patricia Kayal, Philip's sister-in-law, perfected this recipe after a losing bou with the munchies. They make a perfect shovel for any dip, especiall *m'hammara* (page 61).

The chips can be stored several weeks in an airtight container.

4 (6-inch) pita loaves
Olive oil or melted butter
Garlic powder
Assorted spices such as za'atar, onion powder, oregano (optional)

Step 1:
Preheat the oven to 350 degrees.

Step 2:
With kitchen shears, trim ¼ inch off the circumference of each pita. Separate the top from the bottom.

Step 3:
Brush the inside of each piece lightly with olive oil or butter and sprinkle garlic powder or assorted spices if desired over them.

Step 4:
With the shears or sharp knife cut each piece in half and then into three or four wedges.

Step 5:
Place the wedges, seasoned side up, on an ungreased cookie sheet and bake 8 minutes or until golden brown. Cool completely on rack before serving.

POMEGRANATE MOLASSES

Dibs Rim'an

Yield: 2 quarts

The old fashioned Syrian way to make this aromatic-cooking base involves cooking down the crushed seeds of two dozen pomegranates. This may be an authentic Syrian cookbook, but we thought you would find the alternate approach offered here a little less intimidating. *Dibs rim'an* provides the flavor that underlays many of our stuffed vegetable dishes. It has a tangy, almost sweet and sour taste, and is used as a base in the tomato and lemon juice mixtures used for stuffed cabbage, eggplant and other dishes. It is also used in *lahem'ajeen*, our delicious meat pie.

Raw pomegranate juice can be purchased in health food or most Middle Eastern stores. You can also buy decent commercial brands of already prepared *dibs rim'an* in any Middle Eastern store or gourmet food shop.

2 quarts (8 cups) pomegranate juice
2 quarts (8 cups) bottled lemon juice
5 pounds sugar
1 tablespoon pectin

Blend the pomegranate juice, lemon juice, and sugar in a 6-quart pot. Cover and bring to a slow boil. Lower the heat and simmer for 2 hours. Mix in the pectin. Continue cooking an additional 2½ hours, stirring occasionally. Turn off the heat and let cool. Pour or spoon into individual canning jars. Cover and refrigerate overnight before using. The molasses will thicken after refrigeration and last at least 1 year.

RENDERED BUTTER

Zibdeh Migleha *Yield: 3¿ cups*

Many of our recipes call for different amounts of rendered butter. No matter how much butter is needed render it according to these instructions. For ease of use and availability, we specify rendering at least 2 pounds of butter at one time. Render the butter at your leisure and refrigerate for later use.

Sitto Helen's trick for "perfect" rendered butter is to blow into the butter after it has simmered for ½ hour. If it separates in the middle and the salt is visible on the bottom, it is just right. If not, continue cooking.

2 pounds (8 sticks) salted butter

Put the butter in a deep pot and cover with lid tilted. Melt on medium/low heat (careful, if the heat if too high the butter will burn). When it becomes foamy and starts to rise lower the heat. Continue to simmer for approximately 40 minutes. Turn off the heat and set aside to cool. Pour through a fine strainer to remove the excess salt.

RICE WITH VERMICELLI

Riz ou Shar'eah *Yield: 6 to 8 servings*

Sitto Helen makes rice with chicken broth, vermicelli and pine nuts. This is always a special and attractive treat.

4 tablespoons salted butter
1 cup fideo/vermicelli-style noodles, crushed
*4½ cups chicken broth**
1 teaspoon kosher salt
2 cups uncooked white rice

Garnish
½ cup pine nuts, lightly toasted

Step 1:
Melt the butter on low heat in a wide, deep pot. Add the vermicelli and stir until golden brown (approximately 5 minutes).

Step 2:
Add the chicken broth and salt, cover and bring to a boil. Mix in the rice and lower the heat. Recover and simmer 30 minutes or until the rice is tender and the broth has evaporated. Keep the pot covered for at least 5 minutes before mixing.

Step 3:
Garnish with pine nuts before serving.

* Normally the measurement for rice is 2 cups liquid to 1 cup of rice. When using vermicelli, it is best to add an additional ¼ cup broth for each cup of rice used.

SUGAR SYRUP

A'ther *Yield: 3½ cups*

Baklava is the most popular dessert using *a'ther*. To save time, prepare the syrup beforehand. It will keep a few months in the refrigerator. If the syrup crystallizes, it can no longer be used.

4 cups sugar
1½ cups cold water
1 tablespoon fresh lemon juice
1 teaspoon rose water (optional)

Pour the sugar, water, lemon juice, and rose water if desired into a medium-size pot. Mix and bring to a boil. Lower the heat and simmer approximately 20 minutes or until slightly thickened.

Use as needed.

SYRIAN RICE

Riz *Yield: 6 servings*

Sitto Alice made only saffron-flavored rice. Given its inflated price, Philip uses turmeric instead. Either way it is easy to prepare and tasty.

4 cups cold water
2 cups uncooked white rice
4 tablespoons salted butter
1 teaspoon kosher salt
Dash of saffron or turmeric

Garnish
½ cup pine nuts, lightly toasted

Step 1:
Boil the water in a wide, deep pot. Add the rice, butter, salt, saffron or tumeric and mix. Cover and lower the heat. Simmer 20 minutes or until the rice is tender.

Step 2:
When the rice is cooked, keep the pot covered for at least 5 minutes before mixing.

Step 3:
Garnish with pine nuts before serving.

TURKISH COFFEE

Ah'weh Turkieh *Yield: 8 servings*

This Turkish "espresso" is now called *ah'weh arabe* and is a must with Syrian pastries. Our family traditionally uses a brass or copper Turkish demitasse pot. These have pouring flanges and extended handles essential for ease of cooking and serving, and can be found in Middle Eastern markets.

In Syria, extra sugar is added to each cup, but not stirred in. Middle Easterners simply love it this way, but American tastes generally differ.

4 leveled teaspoons Turkish or Arabic coffee
2 teaspoons sugar
10 ounces cold water

Utensil:
Turkish demitasse pot or equivalent
8 espresso cups

Boil the coffee, sugar and water in a pot on high heat. Stir constantly with a long spoon. As foam appears remove the pot from the heat and immediately spoon the foam into the espresso cups. Return the pot to the heat for another 1 or 2 minutes, stirring and lifting the pot off the fire to avoid spill. Pour the coffee into the cups. The foam will rise to the top.

YOGURT

Leban *Yield: 2 quarts or 12 servings*

Although commercial yogurts have improved in taste, homemade yogurt is always better. It is also less expensive, smoother, and fresher. The recipe below can be easily halved.

Romi brand yogurt is excellent by Syrian standards and makes for delicious *lebaneh*. Middle Eastern stores carry it and other imported brands that are both rich and tasty. Removing the fat from the top of a whole milk yogurt is one way of getting a full flavored yogurt without the added calories. All yogurts can be used as yogurt starters. To improve their catalytic properties you can add an acidophilus capsule. Simply open one, and blend its contents into the starter yogurt (*roh'bier*).

Leban accompanies many dishes and is a primary element in Syrian cuisine. As a summer cooler, it can be eaten alone or mixed with lettuce, diced cucumbers, dried mint and crushed garlic. It also goes well with fruit or topped with granola or any grainy-type cereal. Many times we just enjoy pita dipped in *leban*.

2 quarts whole milk
8 ounces plain yogurt for starter, stirred

Step 1:

Heat the milk in a deep pot, on medium heat, stirring occasionally at first until the milk rises (10 to 12 minutes). Be careful, milk boils faster than water and can burn easily. Remove from the stove immediately after it rises, stir, and set aside. When the milk cools (approximately 30 minutes) add the yogurt and mix thoroughly, but gently.

For perfect *leban*, our Sittos would stir the hot milk occasionally after removing it from the stove and test its temperature by slowly counting to ten while immersing a pinky finger in it. When they were able to withstand the heat, it was cool enough to add the yogurt starter.

Continued

Step 2:

Pour the milk and starter mixture into a 2-quart jar or a wide plastic container.* Cover tightly and set aside. Cover with a heavy cloth or towel and leave undisturbed for at least 5 hours or overnight. You can also place the *leban*, sans towel, undisturbed on a rack in the oven if it has a continuous pilot flame. In either case, do not touch it for at least 5 hours. Then, refrigerate at least 5 hours before serving.

*If using a wide container (before refrigerating) place a sheet of paper towel on top of the *leban* to remove excess moisture. Cover tightly and refrigerate. Remove before serving.

YOGURT DRINK

Leban Shrub'eh *Yield: 1 serving*

For Syrians, this is the ultimate cooler on a hot summer night.

4 ounces plain yogurt
3 ounces cold water
1 teaspoon dried mint
1 small clove garlic, crushed (optional)
4 ice cubes

Mix the yogurt and water in an 8-ounce glass. Add the mint, garlic and ice cubes and gently mix again.

This drink can also be store bought, but it will never be as good as your own. Drink and enjoy!

Desserts, Pastries, and Cookies

(Hilweh)

BAKLAVA

Batlawa *Yield: approximately 100 pastries*

Baklava, or *Batlawa*, as it is known in Arabic, is probably the best-known dessert served in Middle Eastern homes today, especially during the holi-ays. It presents itself beautifully on a tray wrapped in decorative cellophane nd tied with holiday ribbons. It makes a great hostess gift.

here are different variations on the baklava theme. We use only fillo dough, ugar syrup, butter, and walnuts, while other ethnic groups add cinnamon nd rose water. Though the amounts of sugar and butter may seem large, we ave actually reduced them to lessen the sweetness and caloric content.

/e suggest preparing the walnuts, sugar syrup, and butter beforehand.

aklava can be made either flat and cut diamond shape or round, as a finger-hape pastry. Both are illustrated below. This pastry freezes well, but we don't ave to tell you it tastes best freshly made.

ecipe and ingredients on following page

Flat/diamond shape

2 pounds walnuts, chopped medium/fine
2 tablespoons sugar
2½ cups plus 3 tablespoons melted rendered butter (page xx)
2 pounds #4 fillo dough, at room temperature*
2¾ cups sugar syrup (page xx), at room temperatur

**Use one pound for the bottom layer and the other fc the top. If you prefer a thinner baklava, use one pound fillo; halve all ingredients and use a smaller pan, preferably 9 x 13 x 2-inch.*

Utensils

One 13 x 17-inch pan, or one 15-inch round pan, a least 1½-inches deep
Pastry brush
Paper baking cups

Step 1:

In a bowl, mix the walnuts, sugar, and 3 tablespoons butter. Set aside.

Step 2:

Brush the pan lightly with the butter.

Open one package of dough and lay the sheets flat. Cover with plastic wrap to keep moist. Place 3 sheets of dough atop each other on the bottom of the pan. If using a round pan, alternate them so the entire botton is covered. Tuck in the corner ends. Brush the top of the third sheet lightly with butter. Repeat the process until the entire package is used making sure that every third sheet is buttered. Lightly butter the entire top sheet then spread the walnut mixture evenly over it. Press the nuts down with your hands. Repeat the entire process with the second package of dough until all the sheets are used but do not butter the last 3 sheets.

Step 3:

Preheat the oven to 350 degrees.

Step 4:

Using a sharp knife cut lines deep into the pastry the entire length of the pan 2-inches apart. Then, cut slits about 1¾ inches apart diagonally across the entire pan to produce diamond-shape pieces. Dust your fingers with flour if they stick to the sheets. Pour the remaining butter evenly over the top of the sheets and bake on the middle rack in the oven for 1½ to 2 hours or until the entire top is golden brown. Remove the pan from the oven, set aside to cool for 15 minutes, then pour the sugar syrup evenly over it.

Let cool a few hours or overnight. The pieces will pull apart from each other. Using a sharp knife cut around each piece. Remove each pastry and place in individual paper cups.

Round finger shape

Yield: 60 to 70 pastries

Duplicate the ingredients for flat/diamond shape baklava (page 198)

Step 1:

Brush 2 baking pans lightly with rendered butter and set aside

Step 2:

In a bowl, mix the walnuts, sugar, and 3 tablespoons butter. Set aside.

Step 3:

Open one package of dough and lay the sheets flat. Cover with plastic wrap to keep moist. Carefully place three sheets of dough atop each other lengthwise on a large cutting board. Butter the top sheet lightly. Place approximately 4 tablespoons of walnut mixture along the short side of the sheets but not at the very end or to the edges. Pack the nuts tightly together and fold the sides of the sheets over them. Roll up all 3 sheets tightly, but carefully, so the dough does not rip. As you approach the end of the dough, brush it lightly with butter and roll to completion. Repeat until all of the sheets are used.

Continue with the second package of dough until all the sheets are used.

Continued

Step 4:

Preheat the oven to 350 degrees.

Step 5:

Slice each roll slantwise with a sharp knife, creating individual pieces approximately 2-inches long. Place on a lightly buttered, shallow baking pan, seam side down. Brush the tops generously with butter and place on the middle rack in the oven. Bake for 30 to 40 minutes or until golden brown on top and bottom. Do not turn over. Remove the pans, and set aside for ten minutes. Put approximately 3 tablespoons of sugar syrup on top of each pastry. Place in baking cups.

If you prefer baklava sweeter, add more syrup.

BUTTER COOKIES

Gh'raybeh *Yield: approximately 65*

Gh'raybeh, Sitto Helen's specialty, is a delicate, cookie-like creation that, when made correctly, really does melt in your mouth. Its texture and buttery taste produce a warm and mellow reaction in anyone fortunate enough to sample one. Other family members make excellent *gh'raybeh*, but Sitto's is simply the best.

2¼ cups melted rendered butter (page 186)
1-pound box pure cane superfine, instant dissolving sugar
½ cup semolina
3¾ cups all-purpose flour
4 ounces almonds, skins removed and split

Step 1:

In a bowl, slowly mix the butter for two minutes or 100 times with your fingers. This is how Sitto Helen does it. Add the sugar and mix; add the semolina and mix; add the flour and mix again.

The contemporary approach, of course, would be to use a heavy-duty mixer. Virginia convinced Sitto Helen to try this modern method and, to her surprise, the dough turned out fine. Beat the butter first on low speed then slowly add the remaining ingredients. Mix until well blended.

Test the consistency of the dough by rolling a piece back and forth. The dough should hold together and roll smoothly. If it does not, refrigerate for 10 minutes and try again. If the dough seems too soft when rolling, return to the bowl and add a few tablespoons of flour. If the dough cracks add a little butter, but be careful, if you add too much the finished product will melt into one very large cookie.

Step 2:
Preheat the oven to 250 degrees.

Step 3:
Take a piece of dough, the size of a small egg, and roll back and forth on a flat surface into a cigar shape, about 5-inches long. Form the dough into a pear shape with the sides of your hands and gently press an almond onto the opposite ends. Pick up each one carefully by the narrow end and place on an ungreased baking sheet. Bake 2 hours until lightly golden on top, remove the trays from the oven, and set aside. Do not pick up the cookies for at least 4 hours, then slide a thin spatula under the whole cookie to remove.

COCONUT/WALNUT CAKE

Hareeseet il Loze *Yield: Approximately 28 portions*

If you like coconut, you will love the Syrian version of this American favorite. When preparing the sugar syrup for this recipe, add 2 teaspoons of rose water to the mixture while simmering.

2 cups semolina
1 cup sugar
1 cup flaked coconut
1 cup whole milk, at room temperature
½ cup (1 stick) salted butter
2½ tablespoons baking powder
2 teaspoons pure vanilla extract
1 cup walnuts, chopped medium
1 cup sugar syrup (page 188)
2 teaspoons rose water

Step 1:
In a bowl, mix the semolina, sugar, coconut, and milk. Let it rest for one hour at room temperature.

Step 2:
Preheat the oven to 350 degrees.

Step 3:
Put the butter into a 9 x 13 x 2-inch baking pan and warm in the oven for 5 minutes or until the butter melts. Remove the pan and swirl to coat the entire bottom and sides with the butter. Pour the excess or remaining melted butter on top of the semolina mixture. Mix and add the baking powder. Mix again; add the vanilla; mix and fold in the walnuts. Pour the mixture into the baking pan.

Step 4:
Bake on the lower rack in the oven for 30 minutes or until the edges start to brown. Then, place the pan on the upper rack and bake until the entire top is golden brown. Remove from the oven and immediately pour the sugar syrup over the entire cake. It is best to refrigerate a few hours or overnight before cutting into diamond-shape pieces (see baklava, page 197).

DATE COOKIES

Ca'ak Bil Adg'weh *Yield: 60 to 70*

Rose water gives this dessert an aromatic sparkle. Of course, date pastries are great to begin with. Serve plain or sprinkle lightly with confectioners' sugar.

2 (13-ounce) packages pitted pressed dates
1 cup walnuts, coarsely chopped
2 cups plus 3 tablespoons melted rendered butter (page 186)
Rose water
4 cups all-purpose flour
2 cups semolina
½ cup sugar
2 tablespoons mahlab
2 extra-large eggs, slightly beaten
½ cup whole milk, at room temperature

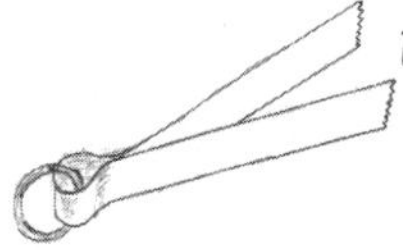

Utensil
Middle Eastern pastry tweezer or any straight-edge tweezer

Step 1:

After checking for pit particles, mix the dates, walnuts, and 3 tablespoons butter in a bowl. This can be quite messy so you may want to use disposable gloves (rub lightly with butter).

Put a generous amount of rose water in the palm of your hand. Take a quarter-size piece of the date mixture and roll it back and forth to a 3-inch length. Set aside. When you are finished with all the dates, lightly rub additional rose water over the tops.

Step 2:

In a bowl, beat the flour, semolina, sugar, and mahlab. Add the eggs, milk, and 2 cups butter and beat again. The dough should be soft and buttery. Any leftover dough can be used to make *ma'moul* (page xx).

Step 3:

Preheat the oven to 350 degrees.

Step 4:

Roll a piece of dough the size of a small egg into a pinky shape about 3½-inches long. Flatten the middle lengthwise; place a date on it, and close the dough around the date. Smooth out and roll back and forth until the date is completely covered. Place on ungreased, shallow baking pans and pinch a design into the tops with the tweezers.

Bake on the bottom rack for approximately 40 minutes or until golden brown on top and bottom. Do not turn over.

A delicious accompaniment to Turkish coffee.

FARINA PUDDING

Batlawa Franjea *Yield: 40 pieces*

Because of its creamy texture, this dessert is an old-time favorite, especially with Sittos' children, grandchildren, and great-grandchildren.

The pudding must be prepared the day before baking in order for it to set. Also, while it is cooking, you **must** keep stirring the pudding until it thickens. If you do not, it will get lumpy.

If preparing for a dinner party, individual, fully cooked portions can be placed on a decorative ovenproof platter beforehand. Just reheat and serve warm.

If you wish to make a smaller portion, use 2 quarts milk, ¾ cup farina, ¾ stick butter, and remaining ingredients as indicated. Also, use a smaller pan but bake the same amount of time.

½ cup (1 stick) salted butter
3 quarts whole milk, at room temperature
2 extra-large eggs, slightly whipped
1½ cups enriched farina (original creamy hot wheat cereal)
¾ cup sugar
2 tablespoons pure vanilla extract

Garnish
Sugar
Cinnamon

Step 1:

Put the butter in a large baking pan approximately 16 x 11 x 2-inch and place in a 300 degree oven for 5 minutes or until the butter melts. Remove the pan and set aside until it cools. Refrigerate to re-harden the butter.

Before beginning Step 2, remove the pan from the refrigerator and set aside.

Step 2:

Pour the milk and eggs into a 5-quart pot. Cook on medium/high heat approximately 10 minutes, stirring every few minutes until the mixture gets hot. Lower the heat to medium and slowly pour in the farina, stirring constantly. Continue cooking an additional ten minutes; pour in the sugar and stir until the mixture gets very thick and feels heavy. This should take approximately 10 to 15 minutes longer. Remove the pot from the stove; add the vanilla and mix well. Pour into the baking pan and set aside until completely cooled. Cover with waxed paper or clear plastic wrap and refrigerate overnight.

Step 3:

Preheat the oven to 350 degrees.

tep 4:

Remove the pudding pan from the refrigerator and cut into diamond-shape pieces, (see baklava, page 197). Bake uncovered, on the lowest rack, 1½ to 2 hours or until golden brown on top. After baking, remove the pan from the oven and set aside for at least 30 minutes before cutting through again to fully separate the pieces.

To serve, place individual pieces on a platter, sprinkle lightly with sugar and cinnamon.

FILLO FILLED WITH PISTACHIOS

Swad el Sit *Yield: approximately 24 pastries*

Similar to Baklava, this flaky delicacy is also referred to as "grandma's bracelets" or "birds' nests." See if there is a resemblance. We think there is.

Prepare the pistachios, sugar syrup and butter beforehand.

1¼ pounds pistachios (skins removed, coarsely chopped)*
1 tablespoon sugar
1 cup plus 2 tablespoons melted rendered butter (page 186)
1 pound #4 fillo dough, at room temperature
1½ cups sugar syrup (page 188) or more, at room temperature
2 teaspoons rose water added to the sugar syrup (optional)

**Walnuts can be substituted for pistachios.*

Utensils
1 wooden stick (⅜-inch diameter and approximately 15-inches long) similar to a dowel
Pastry brush

Step 1:
In a bowl, mix the nuts, sugar, and 2 tablespoons butter. Set aside.

Step 2:
Open the package of dough and lay the sheets flat. Cover with plastic wrap to keep moist.

Place one sheet of dough on a flat surface lengthwise. Place the stick along the wide edge closest to you and roll the sheet around it, leaving a 2-inch flap at the end. Crinkle the dough on the stick by standing it on its end against the work surface and gently pushing the dough down, stopping at the center. Pull out the stick and curve the crinkled dough into a circle in the direction of the flap. The flap will form the bottom of the shell. Place on a lightly buttered, shallow baking pan; brush butter all over the top of the pastry. Continue until all the dough is used.

Step 3

Preheat the oven to 350 degrees.

Step 4:

Fill the shells with approximately 2 tablespoons of nuts and bake 20 minutes or until golden brown on top. While still warm, drizzle syrup over each pastry until completely covered.

FILLO STUFFED WITH RICOTTA

Shibiat *Yield: 18 pastries*

As sweet as baklava, the holidays would not be the same without these triangular-shape goodies.

2 pounds whole milk ricotta
1 pound #4 fillo dough, at room temperature
2 cups melted rendered butter (page 186)
1 cup sugar syrup (page 188)
Cinnamon

Step 1:
Put the ricotta in a wide deep bowl, and press down on the cheese with a few sheets of paper towel to remove excess moisture.

Step 2:
Place the stack of sheets on a cutting board. Cut the stack into 3 equal sections parallel to the short side and place the cut sections on top of each other. Cover with plastic wrap to keep moist. Carefully remove 4 sheets from the stack and place on top of each other on a flat surface. Butter the top sheet and place 1-tablespoon ricotta on the dough 1 inch in from the lower right hand corner. Starting from the left hand corner, fold up the sheets into a triangular shape by crisscrossing each fold as you would a flag. After the last fold, there should be approximately 1-inch dough remaining. Butter lightly, then fold the remaining dough over the pastry. Place seam side down on a lightly buttered, shallow baking pan. Continue until all the sheets are used.

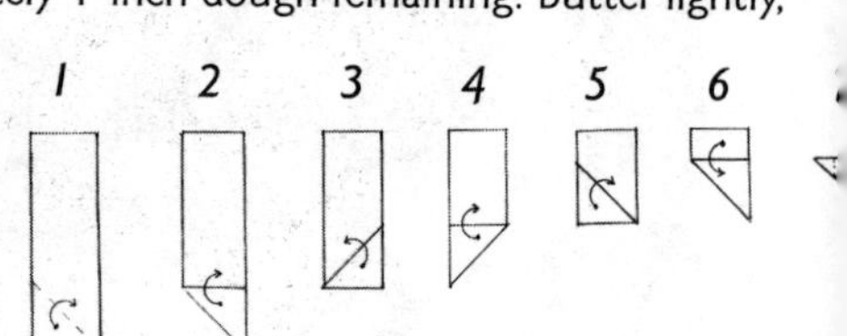

Step 3:
Preheat the oven to 350 degrees.

Step 4:
Butter the tops of the pastries and bake 40 minutes or until the tops are golden brown.

When serving, pour 2 tablespoons of sugar syrup over each pastry and sprinkle lightly with cinnamon.

RICE PUDDING

Riz bil Haleeb — *Yield: 10 to 12*

This is a thick creamy pudding, suitable for family or guests as a snack or dessert.

Riz bil haleeb can be served plain, topped with fresh fruit, or sprinkled with sugar and cinnamon.

2 quarts whole milk
½ cup sugar
½ cup uncooked white rice
1 teaspoon pure vanilla extract

Garnish
Fresh fruit (strawberries, blueberries, raspberries, etc.), diced
Sugar
Cinnamon

Pour the milk into a medium-size, heavy saucepan and heat until warm. Mix in the sugar and rice. Bring to a slow boil; lower the heat and simmer 1 ¼ hours or until thickened. Stir occasionally. When the pudding is cooked, add the vanilla and mix well.

If you prefer a smooth pudding, beat with a hand mixer before serving.

RICOTTA-FILLED PASTRY SQUARES

K'nafeh *Yield: 10 to 12 servings*

So far, we've described many of the desserts in this book as delicious hol day favorites. Redundant, but true, and this one is no different.

1 pound shredded fillo dough
1 cup melted rendered butter (page 186)
2 pounds whole ricotta
¾ cup sugar syrup (page 188), at room temperature

Step 1:

Put the ricotta in a wide deep bowl, and press down on the cheese with few sheets of paper towel to remove excess moisture.

Step 2:

Cut the dough into 1-inch strips and loosely separate. Put in a large bow and pour the butter over it. Mix well by rubbing lightly with the palms o your hands. You might want to use disposable gloves when doing this.

Step 3:

Divide the dough in half. Put one portion into an ungreased 9 x 13 x 2-inch baking pan; spread evenly and press down. Put the cheese over it and spread to the edges of the pan. Put the remaining dough over the cheese, spread evenly and press again. Cover with waxed paper and weig down with heavy objects, such as cans or books. This is to ensure that the dough and cheese are pressed tightly together. Refrigerate overnight and remove the objects before baking.

At this point, *k'nafeh* can be frozen (uncooked) for later use. Simply thaw fully and bake as indicated.

tep 4:

Preheat the oven to 350 degrees.

tep 5:

Cut the dough in the baking pan into 2-inch squares and bake on the bottom shelf for 25 minutes. Move the pan to the top shelf and bake 20 minutes longer or until golden brown. Broil for a minute or so if you like it darker.

tep 6:

Let cool 15 minutes, pour syrup over the top and serve. Refrigerate left-overs. To serve, reheat in a preheated 350-degree oven for 10 minutes or heated through.

ROSE WATER PUDDING WITH NUT TOPPING

Ma'halabia *Yield: 6 to 8 servings*

Sitto Helen loves serving this classic dessert to guests. The taste is uniquely cooling, almost fragrant, and very different from any puddings you hav eaten.

2 quarts whole milk, at room temperature
⅔ cup cornstarch
⅔ cup sugar
1 tablespoon rose water

Garnish
½ cup pistachios, minced

Step 1:
Pour the milk into a deep pot. Add the cornstarch and mix; add the suga and mix again.

Step 2:
Bring the mixture to a slow boil, stirring occasionally. Lower the heat anc continue cooking until it thickens (approximately 35 minutes). Remove the pot from the stove; add the rose water and mix.

Step 3:
Pour into individual dishes and let cool. Refrigerate for a few hours or overnight before serving. Garnish with pistachios.

SESAME COOKIES

Simsum *Yield: approximately 80 cookies*

These cookies are perfect for dunking so do not make them too large. Kids just love them.

1 pound raw sesame seeds
3 extra-large eggs
2 tablespoons pure vanilla extract
1½ cups sugar
6 cups all-purpose flour
5½ teaspoons baking powder
2¼ cups vegetable shortening, melted
8 ounces whole milk or more as needed.

Step 1:
Put the seeds in a pan and place in 350-degree oven. Brown lightly (approximately 15 minutes). Stir occasionally and be careful, they burn easily. Set aside.

Step 2:
In a bowl, beat the eggs, vanilla and sugar and set aside.

Step 3:
Pour the flour into a mixer bowl and sift the baking powder into it. Add the shortening and blend. Add the egg mixture and beat on low speed until completely blended.

Step 4:
Spray 2 cookie sheets lightly with a canola oil cooking spray and set aside.

Continued

Step 5:

Pour the milk into a bowl and place the pan with the sesame seeds next to it. Take a small egg-size piece of dough and roll back and forth on a flat surface, until completely smooth. Roll in the milk, and then in the sesame seeds, covering completely. Place on the cookie sheet. Repeat the process until all the cookies are made.

Step 6:

Preheat the oven to 350 degrees.

Step 7:

Bake 35 to 40 minutes or until golden brown on top and bottom. Do not turn over.

Cool the cookies thoroughly before removing from the trays.

"S" SHAPE SEMOLINA COOKIE

Shadaka *Yield: 7 dozen cookies*

Virginia's grandchildren love these crispy cookies and there is always a batch in the freezer to accommodate them when they visit.

½ pound (2 sticks) unsalted butter, melted
1 cup sugar
2½ cups semolina
3½ cups all-purpose flour
3 teaspoons baking powder
1 cup warm water
¼ cup rye whiskey
¼ cup olive oil
2 egg whites

Step 1:
In a bowl, blend the butter and sugar. Add the semolina and flour and beat. Mix the baking powder with the water and add to the bowl. Add the whiskey and oil and mix well. Use the dough immediately

Step 2:
Roll 3 mothball-size pieces of dough into pencil-thin pieces approximately 3-inches long. Lay all 3 alongside each other, press tightly together and shape into an "s." Squeeze each end to keep the pieces together. Place on ungreased baking trays.

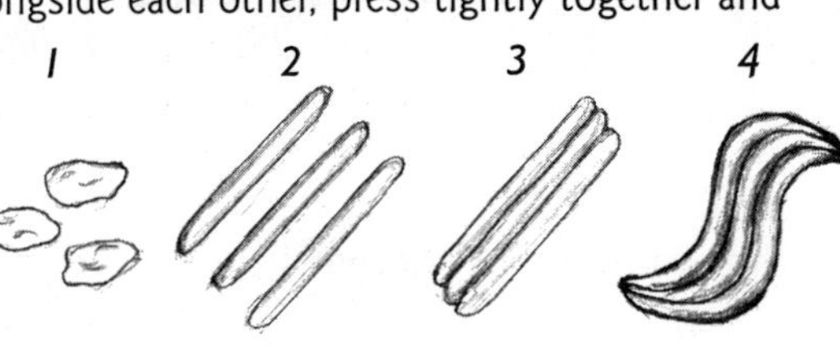

Step 3:
Preheat the oven to 350 degrees.

Step 4:
Brush each cookie generously with the egg whites and bake 40 minutes or until golden brown on top and bottom. Do not turn over.

When the cookies are finished turn off the oven, put them all on one tray and put back in the oven for 1 hour to crisp.

SUGARED WHOLE WHEAT TOPPED WITH POMEGRANATE

Slee'ah *Yield: 20 or more servings*

This healthy, high fiber dessert is usually prepared in the cooler months when pomegranates are available. It is also served at special occasions such as St. Barbara's feast day or the arrival of a baby's first tooth.

Virginia enjoys *slee'ah* as a luncheon entrée, so try it, you might like it too.

This recipe will feed approximately two dozen adults (and fewer children), but you can vary the quantities (proportionately of course) as you wish.

½ cup fennel seeds or to taste
2 pounds whole wheat kernels
1 cup sugar
1 tablespoon cinnamon
1 pound golden raisins
1½ ounces anise seed (multi-colored and candy coated)
½ pound walnuts, lightly toasted

Garnish
1½ ounces anise seed
½ pound walnuts, lightly toasted
Seeds from 6 pomegranates

Step 1:

Preheat oven to 350 degrees.

Put the fennel seeds in a pan and lightly toast in oven for 5 to 7 minutes. Keep mixing to prevent burning. Put into a processor and blend until the consistency is fine and powdery. Measure 3 tablespoons for the *slee'ha* and save the remainder for future use.

Step 2:

In a large deep pot, cover the wheat with water and bring to a boil. Lower the heat, cover with lid tilted and simmer until the kernels are tender. This should take 2½ to 3 hours. When the water starts evaporating, add more. It is important that water covers the wheat at all times for it to cook thoroughly.

Step 3:

After the wheat is completely cooked reserve 1 cup of water and strain the wheat through a colander. Pour the reserved water and the wheat into a large bowl. While still warm add the sugar, cinnamon, raisins, fennel, anise seeds, and walnuts. Mix well and put on a serving platter. Garnish the top with remaining anise seeds, walnuts, and the pomegranate seeds. Leftover dessert should last a week refrigerated.

Although it is a dessert, *Slee'ah* can be eaten anytime of the day.

VANILLA CUSTARD

Crema *Yield: 15 to 20 servings*

This light dessert is perfect during the holidays. We recommend preparing the custard a day before serving in order for it to set.

3 cups sugar
2½ quarts whole milk
10 extra-large eggs
2 teaspoons pure vanilla extract
1 teaspoon cream of tartar (optional)
½ cup walnuts or pistachios, chopped

Step 1:

Put 2 cups sugar in a heavy saucepan and melt on low heat, stirring frequently. Be careful, sugar burns quickly. Once the sugar melts and darkens to a butterscotch color, immediately transfer to an ovenproof bowl.* Hold the bowl with pot holders and swirl the sugar until the sides and bottom are coated. You may hear crackling but, do not fret, it is not the bowl cracking, it is the sugar.

*If some of the sugar hardens in the saucepan while pouring into the bowl, put the pan back on the stove, melt the remaining sugar, and repeat the above process.

Step 2:

Pour the milk into a saucepan and add 1 cup sugar. Mix and bring to a slow boil. Remove from the stove and cool.

Step 3:

Preheat the oven to 350 degrees.

Step 4:

Crack the eggs into a mixing bowl and add the milk mixture and vanilla. Beat on medium speed for 2 minutes. Strain into the glazed bowl; cover with foil and set aside. Pour water into a round baking pan (large enough to hold the bowl) to a 1-inch depth. If using an aluminum pan, add the cream of tartar if desired so the pan does not turn black, and mix. Place the bowl in the water bath.

Step 5:

Place the pan in the oven on the middle rack and bake 15 minutes. Remove the foil and continue baking 1 hour. Change the oven temperature to 400 degrees and continue baking an additional 15 minutes or until the custard is browned on top. Remove the pan from the oven and set aside to cool thoroughly. Remove the bowl, dry the bottom, and refrigerate overnight.

Step 6:

Before serving, garnish with walnuts or pistachios and spoon the custard into individual dishes. When you remove some custard, the browned sugar will rise to the top. Spoon some extra sugar syrup onto the top of each portion.

WALNUT-FILLED PANCAKE TURNOVERS

Atha'yaf *Yield: 25 to 30 turnovers*

These turnovers are also delicious filled with ricotta. The variation is given below. We usually fry these holiday turnovers immediately before serving but if you are serving to guests, it might be more convenient to cook them a few hours in advance. If this is your intention, fry until lightly browned since the pancakes are going to be reheated before serving. Keep at room temperature, reheat in a 350 oven for 10 minutes, and serve.

Experience has taught us that *atha'yaf* simply works best with Aunt Jemima's pancake mix. We have no idea why, but every time we tried using different brands the outcome was disappointing.

2 cups Aunt Jemima's "original" pancake mix (exclusively)
2¾ cups cold water
2 pounds walnuts, chopped, medium/fine
Canola oil
Vegetable shortening
Sugar syrup (page 188), at room temperature
Cinnamon

Step 1:

Blend the pancake mix with the water. Use right away so it doesn't thicken. If it does, add additional water. The batter works best when it is slightly thin.

Step 2:

Pour enough batter onto a lightly buttered, heated pancake grill or into a large frying pan to make a pancake 4 inches in diameter. Make only 3 to 4 pancakes at a time. Do not turn the pancake over. When it bubbles and the top is almost dry remove. Place the pancake on a sheet of paper towel.

Step 3:

Holding a pancake in the palm of your hand, place 1-tablespoon walnuts in the uncooked middle. Fold carefully and press the edges tightly together. Set aside.

If you do not intend to use the stuffed pancakes immediately, you can freeze them. Do not overlap when putting in a freezer container and cover each layer with waxed paper before sealing. Do not thaw the turnovers when you are ready to fry them. Follow directions below.

Step 4:

Fry in an even mixture of oil and shortening (enough to cover the bottom of the pan) until golden brown on both sides. Use a slotted spoon to turn and remove. Drain well on paper towels.

Step 5:

Soak the turnovers in a bowl of sugar syrup. Serve on a platter and sprinkle with cinnamon.

Ricotta-Filled Pancake Turnovers

Use 2 pounds whole ricotta instead of the walnuts. Place the ricotta in a wide deep bowl and press down on the cheese with a few paper towels to remove excess moisture. Spoon it in the pancakes as you did with the walnuts in Step 3. You can also fill half the pancakes with walnuts and the other half with ricotta.

WALNUT-STUFFED PASTRY TOPPED WITH MARSHMALLOW

Cara'beech — *Yield: 70 to 80* cara'beech *or 40 to 50* ma'moul

This elegant pastry can be your *tour de force* when serving company. These cookies are topped with *natif*, a white marshmallow-like sauce that makes a beautiful cover when accented with cinnamon. A variation of this recipe, *Ma'moul*, is given below.

4 cups semolina
2½ cups all-purpose flour
2 cups and 3 tablespoons melted rendered butter (page 186)
1 cup warm water
1 pound walnuts, chopped medium/fine

Garnish
natif *(recipe follows)*
Cinnamon

Step 1:
In a mixing bowl, beat the semolina, flour, and 2 cups butter on low speed. Add the water and beat again. Cover and set aside for 2 hours at room temperature.

Step 2:
Mix well the walnuts and 3 tablespoons butter. Set aside.

Step 3:
Preheat the oven to 350 degrees.

Step 4:
In a walnut-size piece of dough, make a depression with your thumb large enough to hold 1 teaspoon of the nut filling. Insert the filling and push down slightly. Pinch to close and carefully roll the dough in the palms of your hands until it is egg-shaped and smooth, and the opening is completely

sealed. Place the cookies on ungreased baking trays and bake for 30 to 35 minutes or until golden brown on the bottom.

Ma'moul

Ma'moul is a sugar-coated walnut cookie. Ingredients and preparation are exactly the same as *cara'beech* but *natif* is not used. These cookies are made slightly larger and the tops are designed with a Middle Eastern tool, similar to a tweezer. Instead of a topping of *natif*, a generous amount of confectioners' sugar is sprinkled over the top of each cookie after baking.

Natif

Yield: approximately 6 cups

Halva root, imported from Syria or "soap bark," as we call it, resembles small pieces of tree bark. It is the main ingredient in our original recipe and can be purchased at many Middle Eastern supermarkets. If you cannot find it, try the alternate recipe below. The finished product resembles marshmallow fluff, a popular American topping, but the consistency of *natif* is slightly thicker. *Natif* can also be frozen. Just thaw and mix well before using.

Original recipe:

1/4 pound halva root
2 cups cold water
4 cups heavy sugar syrup (page 188), heated slightly*
2 egg whites, stiffly beaten
3 drops rose water (optional)

**To make heavier syrup, simmer an additional 10 minutes.*

Step 1:

Pound the halva root into small fragments and put in a small saucepan. Cover with the cold water and bring to a boil. Lower the heat and simmer 20 minutes. Strain and reserve 1 cup of the liquid. Discard everything else.

Continued

Step 2:

In a mixer bowl, whip the cup of *halva* liquid on high speed until rich foam appears. Add the sugar syrup, egg whites, and rose water (optional) and continue mixing until it is thick and creamy. Pour into a bowl and use immediately or refrigerate/freeze for later use.

When ready to serve, put one teaspoon of *natif* on each cookie, stack on a serving dish and sprinkle with cinnamon.

Alternate recipe:

Yield: approximately 6 cups

2½ cups sugar
1 cup cold water
1 tablespoon fresh lemon juice
3 egg whites
½ teaspoon cream of tartar

Step 1:

Mix the sugar, water and lemon juice in a saucepan and bring to a boil. Lower the heat and simmer 15 minutes, stirring occasionally. Turn off the heat, cover, and set aside.

Step 2:

In a mixing bowl, beat to stiff peaks, on high speed, the egg whites and cream of tartar. This should take approximately 5 minutes. Blend the hot syrup slowly into the egg mixture and beat an additional 10 minutes or until thickened and fluffy.

Pour into a bowl and use immediately or refrigerate/freeze for later use.

Arabic Index

Index

M:

N:

Y:

From Hippocrene's

COOKBOOK LIBRARY

A TASTE OF TURKISH CUISINE

Nur İlkin and Sheilah Kaufman

The traditional dishes featured in *A Taste of Turkish Cuisine* make use of a variety of beans, grains, fresh fruits, vegetables, herbs, and, of course, yogurt, one of Turkey's most important contributions to international cuisine. Simple yet rich in flavors, Turkish cuisine resounds of its varied influences, which range from Chinese and Mongolian to Persian and Greek.
A history of Turkey's culinary traditions accompanies the 187 recipes, as well as glossaries of commonly used ingredients and Turkish cooking terms.

TWO-COLOR • 273 PAGES • 6 X 9 • 0-7818-0948-7 • $24.95 HC • (392)

THE ART OF TURKISH COOKING

Neşet Eren

Paperback edition of the 1969 classic.

308 PAGES • 5½ X 8½ • 0-7818-0201-6 • $12.95PB • (162)

SEPHARDIC ISRAELI CUISINE:
A Mediterranean Mosaic

Sheilah Kaufman

Sephardic, derived from the Hebrew word for Spain, defines the Jews of Spain, Portugal, North Africa and the Middle East. The foods of these Mediterranean countries profoundly influenced the Sephardic Israeli cuisine, which abounds with ingredients such as cinnamon, saffron, orange flower water, tahini paste, artichokes, fava beans, couscous, bulgur, persimmons, peaches, and limes.

Sephardic Israeli Cuisine offers 120 kosher recipes that celebrate the colorful and delicious culinary mosaic it represents. Using typical Sephardic ingredients, it includes favorites like Yogurt Cheese; Crescent Olive Puffs; Harira; Tamar's Yemenite Chicken Soup; Grilled Fish with Chermoula; Moroccan Cholent; and Moroccan Sweet Potato Pie.

264 PAGES • 5½ X 8½ • 0-7818-0926-6 • $24.95HC • (21)

CUISINES OF THE CAUCASUS MOUNTAINS

Recipes, Drinks, and Lore from Armenia, Azerbaijan, Georgia, and Russia

Kay Shaw Nelson

People of the Caucasus Mountains, a region comprising Armenia, Azerbaijan, Georgia and Russia, are noted for a creative and masterful cuisine that cooks evolved over the years by using fragrant herbs and spices and tart flavors such as lemons and sour plums. The 184 authentic recipes featured in *Cuisines of the Caucasus Mountains* offer new ways of cooking with healthful yet delectable ingredients like pomegranates, saffron, rose water, honey, olive oil, yogurt, onions, garlic, fresh and dried fruits, and a variety of nuts. The literary excerpts, legends, and lore sprinkled throughout the book will also enchant the reader-chef on this culinary journey to one of the world's most famous mountain ranges.

288 PAGES • 6 X 9 • 0-7818-0928-2 • $24.95HC • (37)

AFGHAN FOOD & COOKERY

Helen Saberi

This classic source for Afghan cookery is now available in an updated and expanded North American edition! This hearty cuisine includes a tempting variety of offerings: lamb, pasta, chickpeas, rice pilafs, flat breads, kebabs, spinach, okra, lentils, yogurt, pastries and delicious teas, all flavored with delicate spices, are staple ingredients. The author's informative introduction describes traditional Afghan holidays, festivals and celebrations; she also includes a section "The Afghan Kitchen," which provides essentials about cooking utensils, spices, ingredients and methods.

312 PAGES • 5½ X 8¼ • ILLUSTRATIONS • $12.95PB • 0-7818-0807-3 • (510)

EGYPTIAN COOKING

199 PAGES • 5½ X 8½ • ISBN 0-7818-0643-7 • NA • $11.95PB • (727)

TASTES OF NORTH AFRICA

Recipes from Morocco to the Mediterranean

160 PAGES • 5½ X 9½ • 23 FULL PAGE COLOR PHOTOGRAPHS • ISBN 0-7818-0725-5 • NA • $27.50HC • (187)

From Hippocrene's
ARABIC LIBRARY

ARABIC PROVERBS
Joseph Hanki

First published in Egypt in 1897, this recent addition to the Hippocrene bilingual collection of proverbs contains 600 Arabic proverbs written in romanized colloquial Arabic with side-by-side English translations and, where appropriate, explanations of the custom that gave rise to the proverb.

144 PAGES • 6 x 9 • ISBN 0-7818-0631-3 • W • $11.95PB • (711)

TREASURY OF ARABIC LOVE: POEMS, QUOTATIONS AND PROVERBS
in Arabic and English
Edited by Farid Bitar

This collection of love poems, quotations and proverbs, ranging from the 6th to the 20th century A.D., are given in both Arabic and English. This beautiful, concise hardcover edition makes a perfect gift for the romantic.

128 PAGES • 5 x 7 • ISBN 7818-0395-0 • W • $11.95HC • (71)

ARABIC FIRST NAMES

Out of the extremely rich Arab heritage comes this volume of 600 first names with their meaning and historic origins, ranging from names with religious connotations such as *Abdulhamid*—'Servant of the Praised' to modern names like *Basma*—'Smile'.

100 PAGES • 5 x 7 • ISBN 0-7818-0688-7 • W • $11.95HC • (777)

HIPPOCRENE CHILDREN'S ILLUSTRATED ARABIC DICTIONARY

English-Arabic/Arabic-English

Hippocrene offers a delightful antidote to the assumption that difficult languages cannot be taught in a playful way with this illustrated children's dictionary. Featuring 500 Arabic words in their original spelling along with easy-to-use English pronunciation, this dictionary provides an invaluable basis for learning Arabic at an early age.

500 ENTRIES • 94 PAGES • 8½ x 11 • ISBN 0-7818-0891-X • W • $11.95PB • (212)

ARABIC-ENGLISH/ENGLISH-ARABIC CONCISE DICTIONARY, Romanized

Egyptian and Syrian Dialect

4,500 ENTRIES • 325 PAGES • 4 x 6 • ISBN 0-7818-0686-0 • W • $12.95PB • (775)

ARABIC-ENGLISH/ENGLISH-ARABIC DICTIONARY & PHRASEBOOK

Useful to those traveling throughout the Middle East and Africa, this book presents a standard Arabic and provides both the Arabic script and its romanized transliteration.

50 PAGES • 3¾ x 7½ • ISBN 0-7818-0973-8 • W • $11.95 • (445)

MASTERING ARABIC

Book and Audio Cassettes

20 PAGES • 5¼ x 8¼ • ISBN 0-87052-922-6 • USA • $14.95PB • (501)
CASSETTES: ISBN 0-87052-984-6 • USA • $12.95 • (507)

EMERGENCY ARABIC PHRASEBOOK

This book gives aid workers, students, travelers and foreign dignitaries the essential words and phrases at their fingertips when they need them most.

80 PAGES • 7½ x 4½ • ISBN 0-7818-0976-2 • NA • $5.95 • (467)

SAUDI ARABIC BASIC COURSE

Reflecting a preference for "modern" words and structure, this guide give the student working proficiency in the language to satisfy social demand and business requirements.

288 PAGES • 6½ x 8½ • ISBN 0-7818-0257-1 • W • $14.95PB • (171)

ARABIC FOR BEGINNER'S
Revised Edition

204 PAGES • 5½ x 8½ • ISBN 0-7818-0841-3 • $11.95 • (229)

All prices are subject to change without prior notice. To order HIPPOCRENE BOOKS, contact your local bookstore, call (718) 454-2366, visit www.hippocrenebooks.com, or write to: Hippocrene Books, 171 Madison Avenue, New York, NY 10016. Please enclose check or money order adding $5.00 shipping (UPS) for the first book and $.50 for each additional title.